Tarot

Dynamics

Tarot Dynamics

Published by:

Kima Global Publishers

Kima Global House,

50, Clovelly Road

Clovelly

7975

South Africa

e-mail: info@kimaglobal.co.za

Website: http://www.kimaglobal.co.za

© Anna Burroughs Cook

ISBN 978-0-9814278-2-9

First Edition: March 2009

Cover & book design: Nadine May

Images of the Universal Tarot used with permission of Lo Scarabeo, Italy

Tarot Dynamics

Anna Burroughs Cook

Acknowledgments

I wish to acknowledge the following people whose affection and limitless patience transformed Tarot-Dynamics from a dream into a dream come true.

First of all, my husband, Richard Crombie, for giving Tarot-Dynamics its title, who patiently sifted through reams of text, correcting my grammatical errors and punctuation.

Linton D. Overholt, who taught me how to write when he generously tackled the monumental job of editing the earliest version of Tarot–Dynamics.

Dan Rauch. A computer tech who somehow managed to keep bringing my old computer back to life.

Lily Goudie, Doris Phillips, Sheri Presloid ,Lisa Diane Lubrano, and Sue Rauch , all friends indeed, whose encouragement I could always rely on, and whose patience I sometimes tested.

How could I not say a heart-felt thank-you to thirty years worth of clients from coast to coast for trusting me to tell them the truth – even when it wasn't what they wanted to hear.

Nadine May, who was with me every step of the way in our mad dash to get T-D into print.

Suzy (our spoiled Rottenweiler) Cagney (our good Shepherd) and Buddy (our super Spaniel) just for always making me smile simply by being their irreplaceable selves!

Last but not Least, a warm thank you and welcome, to everyone who is taking the time to read Tarot-Dynamics.

Anna Burroughs Cook

Dedication

This book is dedicated in memory of Eleanor Mannochio

May you have the foresight to know where you're going,

The hindsight to know where you've been,
&
The insight to know where you are.

Irish Proverb

Note from the Publisher

This book is designed to be used with any 78 card Tarot Deck. We encourage you to place your own cards over the images in the book even if they are from another deck. This widens the scope of the book and reinforces your learning experience.

A lot of love and dedication by the author has gone into the making of this book, so we trust that it becomes a faithful companion to you on your Tarot journey.

Table of Contents

Introduction

There are some things that we do not believe unless we understand them, and some things we do not understand unless we believe them.-
Saint Augustin

The accuracy of any forecast from the stock market, to the weather, or the future success of a single individual relies upon the sensitivity and skill of the interpreter. The art of reading the Tarot has been a respected (if somewhat mysterious) form of divination for hundreds of years. There have been many debates about the Tarot's specific origins but its roots can be traced back to one of the original versions found in the Kabbalah, a book of Hebrew traditions and Gnostic knowledge. Tarot Dynamics is intended to be a study guide to help you master the Tarot and develop your own technique for interpreting the cards.

DO'S and DON'TS

DO read this study guide cover to cover and then:

DO memorize the characteristics for the five Tarot suits. Memorizing them in groups of ten worked well for me, but find a way that's comfortable for you.

DO develop your own keywords. How? After having read this book and absorbed its guidelines, sit down with a pen and paper and study the picture of each card in your deck. Write down a keyword that describes what you "feel" when you see that card, anger, enlightenment, success, worry, travel, promotion etc. Use your keywords. Whether or not your definition for a particular card agrees with anyone else's is NOT important as long as the information you provide is correct.

DO be as creative as you wish. Devising your own Tarot spread can be fun.

DO not be surprised, once you've learned to relax, if you discover that doing a reading for someone else is much easier than trying to read a Tarot spread for yourself!

DO you have to memorize the names and numbers of all seventy-eight cards, or devise your own keywords? Not if you don't want to. Memorizing the five keywords for each of the five suits will suffice if you are more curious than serious about learning the Tarot and uninterested in reading any Tarot decks except the one featured in this book.

* * *

DON'T read the cards for yourself unless you're relaxed and in control of your emotions. Otherwise, the cards are more likely to echo your anxiety, which won't help matters.

DON'T do a full reading of the cards for yourself or anyone else too often. I won't read for a client more often than every three to six months. Give matters time to develop. Remember too, that the greater the affection between you and the person you're reading, the harder it is to remain as open and objective as you should be.

DON'T read the cards for other people who are upset. Postpone their reading until they've calmed down. Otherwise, the cards will simply echo their anxiety and your reading will prove inaccurate.

DON'T read the cards for anyone who intimidates you. If your information is inaccurate, they'll never let you forget it. If you're correct, they'll chalk your success up to luck.

After purchasing your Tarot cards

Remove the cards from the box and cellophane wrapper. Shuffle the cards for a few moments making sure you mix them very well before returning them to the box. During the days before you use your cards for the first time, you may either sleep with the box of cards under your pillow or on your nightstand. If your home is your primary base of operations, keep the box of cards near you as you perform your daily routines. Feel free to shuffle them occasionally. This exercise allows you and your cards to become more familiar with one another. However, if you work outside the home, carry them in your purse, or in the case of a man, in a briefcase or lunch pail. After using your cards for the first time return them to the box and select a special spot to store them until the next time you use them. Some people prefer wrapping their cards in a piece of silk or purchasing a special box in which to store their Tarot cards.

Reading the Tarot

The Tarot is like anything else – the longer you work with it the more proficient you'll become. Reading the Tarot also has a tendency to open or expand your intuitive faculties. Yes, you're probably going to be nervous when you begin to read the Tarot. You know yourself best. It may be two weeks or six months before you feel confident enough to do a reading without referring to this manual or notes you've taken. When you do deliver your very first "solo" reading, don't be surprised if the harder you try to recall each keyword, definition or placement title, the less you remember and the more you rely on your own intuition – because that's exactly as it should be!

Every now and then one card will appear in several readings over the course of a year or for several different people in the space of month. The more often one card is repeated in consecutive readings for a person the more valuable that card's definition is to their success or disappointment. In one reading it may represent a matter that they're grappling with, in another it may represent a matter they're avoiding. Each time it appears it will strike you differently, you'll receive and provide a little more insight about the situation. The more often one card is repeated throughout several readings for different people in the course of one week, month, or year the more likely it is that some sort of social or economic trend is either developing or underway in the world at large.

Reading the Tarot for other people

Getting over yourself is the first step to reading the Tarot successfully. The greater your fear of saying the wrong thing, the more likely it is you will. By the same token – the more you think you know, the more you're sure to learn. Until, and unless, you can detach yourself from your ego, worries, or self-doubt, you shouldn't attempt to read the Tarot. Why? Because whenever you do a reading for someone else all your sensitivity and awareness needs to be focused on the other person. Detaching yourself from your own concerns is best achieved by developing and applying your own technique for personal relaxation before doing a reading. If you haven't yet discovered a personal relaxation technique, here's what I'd suggest: Sit quietly with your eyes closed or look out the window. Light incense or a scented candle, listen to soft music, or perform some simple exercises. After the reading, take a moment or two to shuffle your cards before returning them to their case.

Reading the Tarot for people at a distance

Doing a Tarot reading by phone has gained popularity in recent years. If you're the caller, the reader allegedly concentrates upon you, shuffles the cards and proceeds to tell you what you want to hear – which is generally quite different from what you need to know! I have several clients living out of state who call for telephone readings a few times each year. Yet, I would never dream of shuffling cards for them. They each have their own deck of Tarot cards which they shuffle before they call me. Doing this insures that their reading is uncontaminated by any outside influence. It also affords me a clear picture of what they need to know. Then we proceed to lay out the cards together while I record the session. When we're finished, I mail the cassette tape to them for future reference. I suggest this technique for two reasons: First, it lends the reading a personal touch, second, it increases my accuracy.

Reading your own Tarot cards

Doing an accurate reading for yourself requires that you remain neutral and objective. Some people start each day by drawing and interpreting one Tarot card from their own deck, or selecting a one or three card reading from a Tarot Web Site – similar to reading your daily horoscope in the newspaper. It's not often that I read my own Tarot cards, but when I do, I only employ the three-card spread (see Chapter Eight). Whenever I'm seriously in need of insight about a matter, I prefer to consult another Tarot reader. Why? Because, the more significant the situation, the harder it becomes NOT to interpret the definitions according to what I want to be true or fear the most. The same will be true for you.

Once, when I was very new to reading the Tarot, I had a client who appeared in a state of high anxiety. Shortly after I began to read, they began to get agitated. Upon reaching the conclusion, they were quite irritable. Since they were obviously displeased, I declined payment for my services. Nonetheless, I wanted to know how I had offended them. Upon voicing this question, the client haughtily replied that they too read the Tarot. In fact, they read their own cards EVERY day and not one thing I'd told them had appeared in their cards! I was quite surprised when a few weeks later they called again. This time they were upset because my reading proved accurate; they wanted to know if I had jinxed them. I reassured them that I certainly had not jinxed them and gently suggested that perhaps their own emotional strength and intensity had led them to misinterpret when they read for themselves. This story illustrates how reading for yourself can wind up an exercise in hearing what we want instead of what we need to know. Flooding yourself with more information than you can process, is another downside to reading your own cards too often.

Your Tarot-Dynamics definitions

Each definition contains two very important phrases that begin with: The more encouraging (or reassuring) the situation, or, the more challenging (or less reassuring) the situation.

These terms refer to reasons for conducting the reading. If for example, you or the person you're reading has discovered you're in line for a promotion or a new job—that's an "encouraging situation". Receiving good news or coming up with a fresh idea, or experiencing a "hunch" that tells you matters will soon be taking a turn for the better are also good examples of encouraging situations.

Consulting the cards will reveal more of what you need to know about your new hope or endeavor. By the same token, should you or the person you're reading discover you're in danger of being down-sized on your job that's a "more challenging situation". Yet, whether you're feeling less positive, or have recently received unsettling news, consulting the cards can also tell you more of what you need to know concerning alternative options and avenues.

Each definition also contains the words: "The more encouraging the other cards in the spread", and "The more challenging the other cards in the spread". You can determine this more easily by viewing your entire spread to see whether any particular suit or subject card (numbers two through ten) hold a majority. Chapter Eleven offers several examples to assist you.The

Left Pages contain in-depth Tarot definitions while the Right Pages provide a Quick Reference.

A hint of romance

The definition for each Court Card as well as the entire suit of Cups contains an additional subheading (entitled romantically) beginning with the phrase: "Should your spread contain a hint of romance". However, there are no hard and fast rules concerning what "a hint of romance" looks like in the Tarot. You see, whether at the beginning, the middle, or the end each romance and every romantic opportunity is as different as the couples that encounter them.

When the client asks, "Can I expect to meet my true love soon?" differentiating between opportunity and wishful thinking in the cards poses a real challenge. I have found it easier to resolve issues concerning romance, as well as romantic misunderstandings, by viewing the entire spread to determine which, if any, Court Cards happen to fall with, or near cards such as the Lovers, the Empress, the Wheel of Fortune, The Star, or The Fool from Major Arcana as well as the Two, Three, Six, or Ten of Cups.

 Here too, with a little time and practice as your intuition becomes stronger and more reliable you're sure to devise your own guidelines. Whether or not you or the person you're reading is involved in a relationship or hopes to find one, every now and then— you'll get a "feeling" from one or more particular cards or their alignment in your spread that alerts you to an impending change in their (or your) emotional situation, so follow your feelings!!!

Differentiating between a challenge and an inconvenience

No matter how rushed you are, a flat tire is more of an inconvenience than a challenge – unless you lack the skill to change the tire yourself, or the means to purchase a new tire. Yet, by over-coming the challenge of learning to change your own tire, or by re-examining your financial situation, you confront the challenge, and that encourages you to become more resourceful and independent.

Keeping matters in perspective

My favorite definition for the word challenge is; a matter or circumstance that requires our immediate attention. Interviewing for a better job is a personal challenge, but the possibility of landing that job overrides our anxiety concerning the interview. Whether or not it's expected, bad news from a doctor or dentist also presents a personal challenge, but the possibility of feeling better helps counteract any anxiety concerning the upcoming medical procedure. Loss of employment, or an unexpected reduction of income also presents a personal challenge, yet by taking the opportunity to develop marketable skills, or by simplifying our life, the initial challenge may prove to be a blessing in disguise.

Getting ready to read

This book is designed to assist you in expanding your intuitive faculties while mastering the Tarot, in just a short time. The next six chapters provide a comprehensive explanation of the five suits that comprise the Tarot. Before you begin reading, please take a moment to memorize the five characteristics that we will be using to define the five suits.

Major Arcana = Karma (cause and effect)

Wands = Change

Cups = Emotion

Swords = Challenges

Pentacles = Ambition

After reading chapters one through twelve, memorizing the names and numbers of all seventy-eight cards is the next step in mastering the Tarot completely. Working with each suit in groups of five or ten worked well for me. Once you've memorized the names and numbers of one complete suit, test yourself. Take a sheet of paper and write down the number for each card in that suit. Then, fill in the name of each card next to its assigned number and check your notes or study-guide to see how right you are. Working with a study-buddy can also be fun.

Depending upon your schedule, it may take as little as three days or perhaps even a week, but once you can think of a random number, (for example) forty-three, and know that that number IS the Three of Cups you're on your way!

Your final step in mastering the Tarot is also your passport to delivering effortless and accurate readings from any and every seventy-eight card Tarot Deck. Just memorize one simple key-word for each of the five Court Cards and eight subject cards from the Minor Arcana listed in Chapter Two of your Study Guide. Please, don't hesitate to devise your own keywords. For example, in Chapter Two Subject Card Seven is said to represent your personal and professional associations. For the sake of simplicity, you might also choose "relationships." Feel free to be as creative as you wish.

FAQ

Q. Isn't it supposed to mean something when the picture on the Tarot card is upside down?

A. That depends upon the interpretation of your reader. Some readers apply the negative (or more challenging) definition to any Tarot card whose picture is reversed or upside down. Once you begin working with your cards it won't be long before you can recognize the difference between genuine challenges and temporary stumbling blocks or hesitation. In my experience it really doesn't matter, but I prefer to see all the cards right side up. Viewing them in this manner improves my range and accuracy.

Q. Why didn't the Tarot reader tell me as much information as my friend received?

A. There are two parts to the answer.

First: Some people hear more, while some hear less during their reading. Some people are going to be up against a wider variety of issues in the near future. Some are already on the path that's right for them, or their life is currently under better control or more organized.

Second: How often do you have your cards read? No matter how much you may like your reader, the better they get to know you, the harder it is for them to retain their objectivity. It's in your best interest to space your readings at least three if not six months apart.

Q. I went to three different readers in three months and heard three different stories, how do I know whom to believe?

A. Chances are that at least a little something from one or more of those readings will come to pass in time. Nonetheless, you're having your cards read too often! If you were comfortable with all three readers, I suggest that you schedule a return session in another three or four months with the reader who provided the most accurate information. If you weren't comfortable with any of those readers, consider shopping around for a reader who does suit you. That's very important. The more comfortable you and the reader feel with one another the more accurate and informative your session will be.

Q. All my cards were terrific – why didn't anything good happen?

A. Were you relaxed and simply concentrating on pleasant thoughts in general when you shuffled the cards? Or were you wishing really hard for something? Remember there really IS a connection between the cards and the person shuffling them that can't be explained. If you were wishing too hard that something would or wouldn't happen, those thoughts may have contaminated your cards. In other words, your mental intensity may have caused the cards to rearrange themselves in the deck according to what you wanted to see. If this was the case, the next time you meet with your reader relax when you shuffle the cards and don't try so hard. However, if you weren't wishing for anything in particular while you shuffled, did you work with your reading to encourage these brighter episodes to come to pass, or were you just waiting for all the goodness to fall from the sky?

The Major Arcana

Major Arcana - Spiritual Karma

Major Arcana cards test, reward, and replenish your strength of character.

CHAPTER 1

The Major Arcana is the first suit in the Tarot. It contains twenty two (22) cards. When translated from Latin, the name Major Arcana means Big Secrets. Major Arcana cards are like the headlines in a newspaper. Collectively, as well as individually, Major Arcana cards represent spiritual karma, which we are forever resolving, creating and/or re-creating.

The more Major Arcana Cards there are in the spread the more emotionally or spiritually significant this reading will prove to be. Although Major Arcana cards sometimes accompany a surprising situation that requires immediate action, as a rule their influence is more subtle – they signal a turning-point in your perception.

On Page 12 you discovered that the more often one card is repeated in consecutive readings the more valuable that card's definition is to your success or disappointment. This is especially true with Major Arcana cards. Depending upon your situation it's not uncommon for as many as three cards to keep reappearing in consecutive readings. Whether their definitions appear to be encouraging you to pay more attention to a situation or give a more serious consideration to an opportunity, the longer you choose to deny, rather than apply your new awareness the longer matters will either remain the same or in limbo.

Although I have not found that it makes any difference whether the card is upright or reversed some people feel that it makes a great deal of difference. Should you be among them, whenever a card appears in reverse (or upside-down) you'd be wise to warn whomever you're reading that some type of unexpected development is on horizon. While it might represent an upcoming matter beyond their control, they could also become their own worst enemy other by giving up too quickly or pushing themselves, or matters too far!

Card 1 the Magician

You can handle or confront anything. Self-Reliance.

The Magician can help you to help yourself become a hero or a heel in the near future. Your willingness, or refusal, to apply your willpower constructively will reward, or undermine, your progress. You won't be satisfied with giving less than your best now. Your need to prove yourself is very karmic. Each of your decisions and actions are designed to produce a definite effect. Emergencies as well as unexpected developments can create opportunities for you — if you're paying attention. You'll feel ready to handle anything, but be careful not to take on more than you know you can handle comfortably.

The more encouraging the other cards in the spread, the more likely you are to receive some type of recognition or reward for your efforts or services. A subconscious harmony between your intuition and the facts can make you more adept at "sensing" what's going to happen next in matters. The more definite your goals the more resourceful your approach to any obstacle that threatens your progress. Your determination to reach your goals can enable you to handle even the most delicate matters with a gentle detachment – getting to the point without making others feel offended or foolish.

The more challenging the situation or other cards in the spread the more you may need to rely on yourself, and if so learning to, or letting yourself relax may be one of your biggest challenges. Trying to make yourself and everything else so perfect may be preventing you from enjoying your gains and loved ones as much as you deserve to. The greater your success or the closer you come to achieving it the more you may fear it will disappear.

Key word:

Self-Reliance.

Card 1

The Magician

Tip:

If this card appears in reverse (or upside-down) it can signify obsessive self-interest and total disregard for others' opinions, advice or assistance.

Card one means: you are not afraid to stand alone — in fact, you sometimes prefer to do so, and often work best alone.

At your best, by challenging yourself to make your best better you can become as courageous as you are innovative.

Under more stressful conditions however, you become very impatient – even ill-tempered in such a way that you thoroughly undermine matters for yourself.

Card 2 The High Priestess

Your relationships will experience some degree of reconstruction and re-evaluation. Passion.

The High Priestess is capricious. When you're having a good day, you can easily attract positive attention and cooperation. On a bad day, without meaning to or realizing it, you could attract negative attention unless you are careful. During this time period your dreams may become more vivid or precognitive. Your personal and professional relationships (especially but not exclusively with women) will experience some degree of reconstruction and re-evaluation. Your likes and dislikes will be more noticeable. The better you feel about yourself and your life, the better you'll feel physically. The greater your irritation or dissatisfaction with yourself, or matters, the greater your vulnerability to illness, negative thinking and suspicion.

The more encouraging the other cards in the spread, the more reliable your intuition will be. Your desire to understand can make you more tolerant of other's idiosyncrasies. Your knack for making the impossible possible could soon be your key to gaining some type of emotional, material or even medical advantage.

The more challenging the situation or other cards in the spread the more you need to monitor your moods and stick to the facts. Giving the impression that you're saying "maybe" instead of "no", could create unnecessary problems. Your desire to protect your loved ones may be making your relationships more challenging than they have to be. Chance, rather than destiny, may bring a material inheritance your way – but not without strings attached.

Key word:

Passion

Card 2

The High Priestess

Tip:

If this card appears in reverse (or upside-down)

The inability to resist a "little" intrigue could bring more than you are prepared to and able to handle.

Card two means: Subconsciously, if not consciously, your emotions are lending a passionate, even sensual impact that other people can feel and will respond to accordingly.

At your best, you will be uncommonly intuitive and compassionate.

Under more stressful conditions however, you may sometimes change the rules in matters to suit yourself, whether to eliminate an obstacle or to confound anyone that you perceive as competition.

Card 3 the Empress

Can and will enhance your luck, opportunity, and talent if you're exerting honest and practical effort. Success.

The Empress can help smooth or improve your communications and develop new or better connections. Being fond of the optimistic opportunist, she can and will enhance your luck, opportunity and talent as long as you're exerting honest and practical effort. The better you feel about you, the better your chances for attaining personal happiness, professional success or financial ease. The greater your self-doubts, the easier others can and may abuse your generosity or trap you in self-defeating situations. Self-indulgence may become your worst enemy, whether you're eating or exercising too much or too little, or becoming addicted to sex, gambling or substance abuse.

The more encouraging the other cards in the spread, the more likely you are to come closer to achieving your objective – if not actually attaining it. Your perseverance, and unshakable, (though not always unwavering) faith in yourself and your goal may soon light your way to success. Knowing that other people are counting on you can bolster your courage, resourcefulness and self-confidence.

The more challenging the situation or other cards in the spread the more diplomatic you'll need to be but the easier you'll devise effective strategies and achieve small advances that can make big differences in the future. Taking a short break can recharge your energy and renew your confidence in matters you were ready to abandon. Your sense of humor can enable you to go with the flow, until you can turn the tide in your favor.

Key word:

Success

Card 3

The Empress

Tip:

If this card appears in reverse (or upside-down) conceit or apathy could trigger setbacks that put you on a different path than the happier one you envisioned.

Card three means: as long as you've been doing your best you're certain to succeed with the matters that come to mean the most to you.

At your best, whatever the situation your flexible nature enables you to remain focused upon your main objective even when you're confronted by other challenges.

Under more stressful conditions however, self-indulgence could tarnish your reputation and achievements

Card 4 the Emperor

You're going to be a little more self-assertive and direct. Control.

The Emperor intensifies your need to discover the truth in all matters. The manner in which you choose to complete matters and resolve your differences can exert a particularly karmic influence. The more challenging it is to complete matters to your satisfaction and everyone's best interest, the more important it is that you try to do so. Self control and self-discipline are important to success. You may have to, or be asked to take charge of an important matter at work or at home.

The more encouraging the other cards in the spread, the greater your mental energy , but the more demands there may be upon your stamina. You can use your sense of humor to turn your less successful experiences into stepping-stones that inspire and instruct others. Your ability to temper your determination with diplomacy can help you to get further ahead in matters at a faster pace than even you expected! You may become somewhat of a legend or a role-model due to your willingness to do whatever it takes to set matters on course and keep them there.

The more challenging the situation or other cards in the spread the harder it may be to gain control of things at home or work. Whether you're angry or worried, giving into the temptation to make matters move faster than they should or really need to could make more – not less problems for you. An overabundance of intensity or self-righteousness may sentence you to social and emotional isolation. The greater your reluctance to accept a matter you cannot change the easier your inner turmoil can upset your physical well-being in ways, which may not be immediately obvious.

Key word:

Control.

Card 4

The Emperor

Tip:

If this card appears in re-verse (or upside-down) Whatever the situation, you may soon discover that you've never really had quite as much con-trol of matters as you be-lieved.

Card four means: a control issue, at work, home or both may bring your emotions closer to the surface, or cause you to be more protective about matters that impact your sense of be-longing and security.

At your best, you will be ambitious but not greedy– more con-cerned about delegating authority than flaunting it,

Under more stressful conditions however, you may become excessively petty, controlling and demanding.

Card 5 the Hierophant

**Your ability to practice what you preach or believe will be tested.
Contradictory**

The harder you work to overcome your inconsistencies, the more
you'll accomplish. When things are going smoothly you'll become bored and restless. When they aren't, you'll either blow
things out of proportion or refuse to consider alternatives. Your
desire to see the truth becomes a double-edged sword when the
facts conflict with your desire to be the good guy. You hate it
when people don't take you seriously, but sometimes keeping
your promises makes you feel as if your being taken advantage
of. Your professional, family and/or love life are sure to be a little
more adventurous and exciting as well as trying and demanding.
Your ability to practice what you preach or believe will be tested.
Since the Hierophant can warn of an impending scandal, unkind
accusation or rumors that may or may not directly involve you,
you'd be especially wise to choose your lovers and associates
more carefully now, because you'll never extricate yourself or
your reputation from unpleasantness as quickly as you might become involved with it. Meditation, yoga or attending your place
of worship can help tame your inconsistencies.

The more encouraging the other cards in the spread, the easier
you can retain your focus and compromise or relate to other
points of view, enabling you to "spice up" some of your relationships and simplify others.

The more challenging the situation or the other cards in the spread
the more cheated and disheartened you'll feel by outcomes that fail
to meet your expectations. Ongoing inconsistencies in your behavior and communication could prove hazardous to your professional
standing, as well as your emotional happiness. Should your moods
dictate your spending habits money problems may a source of con-
stant concern, whether you've created them or allowed others to create them for you.

Key word:

Contradictory

Card 5

The Hierophant

Tip:

If this card appears in reverse (or upside-down) whatever the situation you would be wise to check and double check your facts before taking matters any farther.

Card five means: conflict between what you feel, what you know and what you want.

At your best, you are free-thinking and free-spirited, with a sharp sense of humor and a contagious nonchalance that can minimize tension wherever you go.

Under more stressful conditions however, you can become vulnerable to reckless – even dangerous behavior.

Card 6 The Lovers

You may meet new people who prove important to your future or reconnect with someone from your past. Harmony.

You need to feel proud of those you love and know that they're proud of you. Your willingness, or refusal, to establish harmony between your ideals and life's realities hold the key to your happiness. Events developing now could enhance your awareness and understanding of others, in addition to your peace of mind.

The more encouraging the other cards in the spread, the more you and other people are likely to enjoy each others' company. The better you feel about yourself the more mutually satisfying all your personal relationships will be and your sense of humor can prevent you from viewing every opinion that clashes with yours as a personal threat or insult. You are sure to feel more playful, adventurous and spontaneous. You may be nominated for an award or promotion, receive a bonus, special recognition, or an apology.

The more challenging the situation or the other cards in the spread, even your best relationships may encounter some strain or tension. Assuming that everyone close to you is as loyal to you, as to their own interests, may be one your biggest mistakes. Once you stop trying to be everything to everyone, or expecting others to be everything to you, the relationships that mean the most to you, will show a marked improvement. Continuing or beginning to repress rather than express your feelings could invite more – not less – trauma into your personal and/or professional life.

Key word:

Harmony.

Card 6

The Lovers

Tip:

If this card appears in reverse (or upside-down) Whatever the situation, your dedication to upholding a commitment promise will be tested.

Card six means: an opportunity to repair whatever needs to be repaired or clarified in the hope that matters will run more efficiently and harmoniously.

At your best, your heightened awareness and understanding of others will also help you to achieve a better understanding of yourself.

Under more stressful conditions however, you may become too subservient to others, too jealous or too certain that your charm alone will convince other people to see matters your way.

Card 7 The Chariot

Travel and communication issues will find you devising and revising your strategies and schedules. Advancement.

Certain events that develop will raise your awareness of the constructive or self-defeating manner in which you're moving through life. At this time, you're as much an emotional catalyst for the other people in your life as they are for you. To retain or establish better control of matters at work and home, you will have to play a dual role of follower and leader. You may even emerge as a follower who is becoming an effective leader or simply more independent. Issues relating to travel – as well as communication – will find you devising and revising your personal, professional and financial strategies and schedules. If you're in the habit of driving too quickly or carelessly, there could be a traffic ticket in your near future – unless you're careful.

The more encouraging the other cards in the spread, the greater your efficiency and leadership will be. Any altercations you might encounter will bring you more opportunity than they will cost you. If relocation or travel is on your agenda now there's likely to be a romantic, adventurous or unusual story behind it.

The more challenging the situation or the other cards in the spread the more concentrated your advancement may need to be. At work and home your patience is sure to be tested whether by annoying delays, miscommunication, mechanical breakdowns or a few medical inconveniences. Confronting the worst in matters, no matter how reluctantly, can help free the best in you.

Key word:

Advancement

Card 7

The Chariot

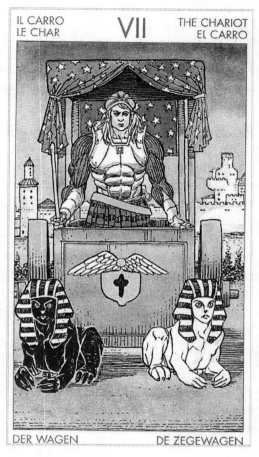

Tip:

If this card appears in reverse (or upside-down) Whether due to circumstances beyond your control or some type of personal miscalculation at work home or both, matters are less likely to proceed as quickly or smoothly as you had hoped.

Card seven means: your attitude, moods and views have a stronger influence upon other people than you may realize.

At your best, whatever the situation, this is time when you can intuitively choose the correct path in every instance and keep matters moving along that path.

Under more stressful conditions however, the more strongly you believe that only one person or matter can make you happy or give your life meaning the more likely you're looking for your self-confidence in the wrong place.

Card 8 Strength

Inner strength can help you meet virtually any challenge – even when you feel unable or you'd rather not try. Renewal.

Summoning your inner Strength will help you combat self-doubt when it threatens your peace of mind and prevent you from creating additional problems through anger, and/or frustration. Letting go of matters you can't change requires more strength than starting over. At this time there is a strong link between your physical and mental health. The stronger you are emotionally, the healthier you'll be physically and the better your chances of minimizing negative effects of minor illnesses. The stronger your motivation, the more vibrant your personality, and the more resourceful your approach to tackling whatever obstacles may appear to be standing between you and your goals.

The more encouraging the other cards in the spread, the more easily your Faith will be rewarded with the peace of mind you deserve, when you know you've done your best. Whatever your situation, now is the time when you can begin to transcend former weaknesses, habits or self-doubts more easily – very much like a butterfly emerging from its chrysalis. Whether or not you've been aware of your intuitive abilities in the past, they may prove uncannily accurate now You may return from a long walk or a short drive feeling completely rejuvenated because the answers you set out to find – found you!

The more challenging the situation or the other cards in the spread the more fears of recrimination, rejection, failure – or being alone – can promote a tendency to settle for what comes the easiest in matters – even when it's not what you want or deserve.

Key word:

Strength

Card 8

Strength

Tip:

If this card appears in reverse (or upside-down) refusing to let go of matters that went wrong in the past could cheat you out of a productive, and happy future.

LA FORZA / LA FORCE — VIII — STRENGTH / LA FUERZA

DIE STÄRKE — DE KRACHT

Card eight means: taking some time-out to recapture or reaffirm your peace of mind and confidence.

At your best, you are more open to exploring new places, methods and ideas in a manner that is as organized as it is realistic.

Under more stressful conditions however, you may sometimes be too quick to blame other people, or see and hear only what you want to.

Card 9 The Hermit

The more you listen, the more you'll learn. Knowledge.

The Hermit can offer you additional spiritual protection while enhancing your awareness or intuition – especially in times of stress or crisis. Taking the time (perhaps through meditation) to integrate your spirituality and intuition could save you from the lesser elements in yourself as well as last-minute physical danger. People's actions will speak to you much louder than their words. The more you listen, the more you'll learn. This is a good time to pursue self-enlightenment whether through private or group study – as a student or even a teacher. The more you rely on your common sense and the less you rely on others to keep their word the more often you'll make the choices and decisions that are best for you and what you hope to achieve.

The more encouraging the other cards in the spread, the easier you can expand your philosophical and intellectual outlook, and plan your advancement in matters. At this time, your ability to sense what other people are about to say or do, may be almost spooky. Your ability to see others, yourself and matters now for what they really are, can help you reach or re-align your goals more quickly and easily.

The more challenging the situation or the other cards in the spread the easier and more effectively you can communicate with people – while keeping your distance and biding your time, much like a general planning a campaign. Your mind is as versatile as it is durable. However, the more attention you devote to one matter, the easier you could lose touch with or track of another.

Key word:

Knowledge.

Card 9

The Hermit

Tip:

If this card appears in reverse (or upside-down) whatever the situation, you may soon be surprised to discover that you don't know quite as much as you believed.

Card nine means: karma (cause and effect) is now working through circumstance to help you tie up any loose ends you've been avoiding.

At your best, you can reduce the most complex data, to something everyone can understand. You're always pondering ways and means to gain additional insight.

Under more stressful conditions however, you will sometimes go out of your way to provoke controversy or a showdown (that you can't win) with other people.

Card 10 Fortune's Wheel

Your attitude and behavior will generate a great deal of "instant karma" that can immediately change the course of matters hanging in the balance. Opportunity.

Fortune's Wheel is a kaleidoscope. When you view matters from one angle, you can see numerous advantages and opportunities through the challenges. Yet, the slightest shift in the angle introduces a completely different picture. Material dilemmas can help strengthen you emotionally and emotional dilemmas can help you become more resourceful materially. Sometimes making the wrong choice may even prove to be the right move that launches you towards victory. The more willing you are to do more than your fair share in matters, the greater your chances of success. The longer you focus on matters that are going against you, the longer it takes to see the opportunities Fortune's Wheel is trying to show you.

The more encouraging the other cards in the spread, the easier you can take charge and make the changes that will make things even better than you expected. The more realistic your goals, the easier you can prevent frustration from running away with your peace of mind. The sooner you utilize your personal strengths, the easier and more quickly you can win against any problems whether you've created them or allowed others to create them for you. When it comes to helping people you care for or blocking your adversaries, you can move mountains now!

The more challenging the situation or the other cards in the spread the more important it is not to punish new opportunities for past mistakes you've made. Fortune's Wheel can enhance your luck in small ways that you may take for granted or consider too insignificant.

Key word:

Opportunity.

Card 10

Fortune's Wheel

Tip:

If this card appears in reverse (or upside-down) a situation or event that doesn't immediately go your way could prove to be a blessing in disguise.

Card ten means: taking a fresh perspective may be your ticket to success by helping you make your best even better.

At your best, you are a self-starter – as confident in your ability to handle your concerns, as you are ready and willing to help others when and where you can.

Under more stressful conditions however, impatience and intolerance for even the kindest suggestions or most constructive criticisms can keep you on the inside track to nowhere.

Card 11 Justice

Justice represents your need to restore or establish better balance in your daily routine. Balance.

You'll need to make certain adjustments, whether to accommodate the unexpected, please yourself and others you care for, or to accommodate a loss. Life is a little less inclined to overlook mistakes you make now. You also may be less tolerant or patient. Justice reminds us that what goes around does indeed come around. In some instances Justice can indicate an approaching (or ongoing) legal concern. As a rule, however, Justice represents your need to restore or establish better balance in your daily routine, whether you've been taking on too much or not enough lately. Consciously, subconsciously, or both, you'll feel more concerned about what's fair for you. In times of trial justice can nudge your conscience and help you make the right decisions – even when you'd prefer not to. However, Justice can sometimes make it more difficult for you apologize or admit your mistakes – it can even render you more vulnerable to manipulation from the people you trust – especially in your family circle.

The more encouraging the other cards in the spread, the easier it will be for you to reorganize your agenda to meet your obligations and insure your peace of mind. The sooner you stop taking yourself for granted the sooner others will too. The better you feel about yourself the less reluctant you'll be to bring any unpleasant episodes to an end. Whatever the situation, the more comfortable you are with yourself and your goals the less you'll worry about making the first move and the less time you'll waste worrying about nonsensical things that could go wrong.

The more challenging the situation or the other cards in the spread the more effort it may require to extricate yourself gracefully from certain issues.

Key word:

Balance.

Card 11

Justice

Tip:

If this card appears in reverse (or upside-down) whatever the situation, a prejudicial attitude coming towards you or from you will only serve to confuse matters.

Card eleven means: taking new matters in stride without unbalancing the other issues in your life.

At your best, no matter how great the temptation, your sense of honesty and fair play will prevent you from committing actions you might later regret.

Under more stressful conditions however, you may be too quick to make mountains out of molehills or take offense where none was intended.

Card 12 The Hanged Man

A positive perspective can help you make more sense of current matters and peace with the past. Tranquility.

The more objectively you view yourself and matters, the more you stand to gain. Retaining an objective attitude now can also boost your physical and emotional defense systems. Consciously, subconsciously, or both, you've been taking a different view of many things, people and yourself that is leading to a spiritual transformation. Your new perspective is helping you make more sense of current matters, helping you make peace with the past and helping you to re-evaluate your goals for the future. You may choose to further your self-enlightenment through group or private study that could include meditation or yoga.

The more encouraging the other cards in the spread, the easier it will be to make realistic decisions and achieve your goals. Tranquility can prevent your spirit from being broken by any setbacks or delays you may encounter. Best of all, people will be unable to make you feel guilty when you know you don't deserve to.

The more challenging the situation or the other cards in the spread the more likely you are to make self-sacrifices that accomplish nothing and prove nothing of value. The greater your self-doubts the more likely you are to follow the path of least resistance; whether or not it's the best path for you or the situation. The easier you can hide your frustration with one matter, the harder it will be to avoid taking out your resentment on other matters and people who don't deserve it. Each loose end that you choose to overlook in one matter, will eventually resurface in another.

Key word:

Tranquility.

Card 12

The Hanged Man

Tip:

If this card appears in reverse (or upside-down) whatever your situation, you may be better prepared to begin taking new steps in a better direction.

Card twelve means: Whatever the situation, you'd be wise to begin (or continue) looking at yourself, matters and others in a manner that is more realistic than idealistic.

At your best, it's impossible for others to make you feel guilty when you know you don't deserve to. You view your best and worst experiences, as friends who help you to bring out the best in yourself and matters.

Under more stressful conditions however, you can submit too quickly and easily to self-limiting habits and attitudes.

Card 13 Death

You're ready for a change. Transformation.

During this time period your past disappointments and successes are signaling a rebirth of your character that can help you triumph over virtually any challenge or tragedy. Whatever the circumstances, you can't function well or happily now in atmospheres that are too stagnant, confining or uncertain. Should it seem that the stronger your desire to succeed the harder it is to decide what you want to do, and where you should begin, by unleashing your ability to separate your feelings from the facts you'll quickly discover that you can make even the most difficult choices and decisions more easily now. This technique can also help ease your mind and clear your conscience of pointless guilt over matters you might have handled differently, even though you know it would not have changed anything for the better.

The more encouraging the other cards in the spread, the more security oriented you are, ready and able to provide your own inspiration and motivation. You're not afraid of compromise and, if necessary you'll work hard to achieve one that's comfortable for all parties. You can end an emotional relationship without sacrificing the friendship or easily resume a friendship from long ago. You're flexible enough to accommodate any unpredictable twists in matters that might arise.

The more challenging the situation or the other cards in the spread, the greater the temptation to dwell upon unpleasant matters, and create excuses that keep you at war with yourself, your opportunities and other people.

Key word:

Transformation

Card 13

Death

Tip:

If this card appears in re-verse (or upside-down) whatever your reasons, the longer you choose to re-main in denial or resistant to making changes that could eventually improve your situation the longer matters will remain in limbo.

Card thirteen means: the greater the challenge, the better the opportunity or the stronger your will to survive the easier you can reinvent yourself– like the Phoenix rising from the ashes.

At your best, you're always open to new ideas and useful in-formation that can help you reach the top in any endeavor.

Under more stressful conditions however, you can be too self-contained– preferring to walk-out instead of talk-out your differences.

Card 14 Temperance

Use your sense of humor to learn from your mistakes. Compromise.

No matter what our goals it's the routines we adopt to achieve them that can literally transform our lives. Compromise is a trait you can't afford to be without – it could even prove to be your Guardian Angel. Physically, the harder it is for you to relax, the more susceptible you may be to mysterious rashes, minor accidents and other annoying more than life-threatening illnesses.

The more encouraging the other cards in the spread, and the more determined you are to win, the more often your fantasies can supply the energy you need to cope when things seem impossible. As you continue to discover and reassemble those "missing pieces" of yourself, your sense of humor can help you realize how your "smaller" trials and tribulations have helped strengthen your character. Whatever the situation, making or taking the time to initiate a frank and open discussion where everyone can "agree to disagree" without endangering their relationship will prevent people from feeling that you are pushing or judging them. If nothing else, clearing the air will ease your mind. You may be pleasantly surprised, to discover that you have been the only person who was demanding too much from yourself.

The more challenging the situation or the other cards in the spread the stronger your temptation to remain chained to people and matters that are wrong for you by telling yourself it's for your own good or the sake of others. Bad relationships can become a bad, but convenient habit – even an excuse for not making the most of yourself and taking your own talents for granted.

Key word:

Compromise.

Card 14

Temperance

Tip:

If this card appears in re-verse (or upside-down) the more likely impulse rather than genuine intu-ition could lead you to say, do or even purchase something you could regret.

Card fourteen means: compromise, with yourself and others' is a trait you can't afford to be without now – it could prove to be your Guardian Angel.

At your best, you're a realist at heart – always ready and eager to expand your horizons, one step at a time.

Under more stressful conditions however, your dreams may prove more precognitive – but difficult to interpret. Whatever your situation, you are likely to be more easily distracted than usual.

Card 15 The Devil

The obstacles confronting you now are more likely to be self-induced. Obstacles.

Whatever your situation – whether you're being tempted or tempting others, the more excuses you make the more obstacles you'll create. Your instincts for emotional and material gain as well as self-preservation are very strong and you must choose whether to let them guide you in the right or wrong direction. If you've been minding your P's & Q's, you're sure to encounter a spot or two of good luck or "flashes" of creative ingenuity that could save you in the nick of time. However, if you've been pushing your luck too far, rather than working through situations, there'll be hell to pay! The obstacles confronting you now are more likely to be self-induced — chiefly promises you've made (perhaps in haste) that you now must live up too. All sorts of mix-ups and inconveniences can arise from nowhere.

The more encouraging the other cards in the spread, the easier you can summon the self-control and self-discipline you need to defeat petty temptations, and perhaps even accomplish the impossible. Common sense can keep your enthusiasm and optimism in check to prevent you from taking on more than you can handle. The more strongly you desire personal recognition or achievement the more accurately you can perceive other peoples' merits and intentions.

The more challenging the situation or the other cards in the spread the greater your susceptibility to procrastination, taking foolish chances, or behaving in a manner that will do you more harm than good. Your desire to be desired or to be of service to others is balanced against a fear of being used – or that other people will expect too much.

Key word:

Obstacles

Card 15

Obstacles

Tip:

If this card appears in reverse (or upside-down)
you may find it easier to
avoid become trapped
by your own or others'
more selfish desires—if
only at the last moment.

Card fifteen means: the stronger your determination to get your
way in matters – the easier you can talk yourself (or anyone else)
into whatever suits your purpose. Whatever your situation, summoning the self-control that you need to defeat petty temptation
now may prove more challenging than you expect.

At your best, your devilish sense of humor and easygoing manner allows you to appear calmer and more confident than you
feel when you're under pressure. Your conscience is a tough task-
master that prevents you from lying to yourself.

Under more stressful conditions however, you can always find
some way to justify your right to do something that you know is wrong!

Card 16 The Tower

Consider reconstructing certain aspects of your life or behavior. Upheaval.

To successfully tie up any loose ends in matters you must be-lieve that your positive efforts are never wasted – even when you don't achieve the results you desired as quickly as you expected. In some manner, your ability to let go of things you still want but don't need will be challenged. Physically you could be your own worst enemy now by neglecting your physician's advice, or waiting too long to seek medical attention. Emotionally, you may need to be a little more flexible to accommodate growing pains in you or your relationships. Professionally and materially, the more you're forced to accomplish on your own now, the more successful you're likely to become. The Tower also champions reconstructing certain aspects of your life or behavior. This is an ideal time to begin rebuilding – from your attitude to your faith, your relationships and everything in be-tween – the right way!

The more encouraging the other cards in the spread, the easier you can tackle self-doubts. You are likely to issue some statements that surprise others. The more you can appreciate knowing the facts in matters now the more quickly and easily you can make whatever changes are necessary to insure your mutual or personal security and continuity.

The more challenging the situation or the other cards in the spread the more likely you are to hear something you won't like, or the harder you may try to hang onto matters that are not as good for you as you're trying to believe they are. A tendency to tell other people only what you feel they need to know could lead to an avoidable misunderstanding.

Key word:

Upheaval

Card 16

The Tower

Tip:

If this card appears in reverse (or upside-down) The longer you continue to focus on only what you wish to see the less satisfied you'll be with everything and everyone else. Refusing to accept things you cannot change, can make you your own worst enemy.

Card sixteen means: an opportunity to begin reconstructing certain aspects of your attitude and behavior that have been preventing you from making the most of yourself.

At your best, the less you can do about one matter – the more strongly you focus on making advancements in others.

Under more stressful conditions however, viewing yourself as a "victim of circumstances" allows you to temporarily ignore the fact that you put yourself in that position.

Card 17 The Star

You're on the verge of a personal transformation. Hope.

You are infused with a conscious and/or subconscious need to know that can help you achieve your goals. Even if it feels as though hope is all you have, it will also be everything you need to motivate yourself. There are billions of stars in the sky. Some glow weakly, some flare brilliantly for a short time and some shine steadily. So it is with you now as you grow in ability, knowledge and understanding. You sense that something is approaching, and you're on the verge of a personal transformation. This is a good time to seek further clarification through meditation, yoga, or attending your place of worship more regularly. Without even trying, you can now draw additional strength and energy from the moods and attitudes of the people who comprise your daily routine. So, the stronger your feelings for them the stronger your intuitive link to them becomes. You may even know when a loved one or friend needs you – before they contact you.

The more encouraging the other cards in the spread, the easier it will be to get in touch with your inner self and allow your intuition to guide you. Your dreams may also reinforce your spiritual/emotional coordination.

The more challenging the situation or the other cards in the spread the more surely you will be tested on your ability to believe that there is a positive purpose behind even the most trying matters. You may seek further clarification through professional counseling.

Key word:

Hope

Card 17

The Star

Tip:

If this card appears in reverse (or upside-down) curiously enough, an unsettling circumstance that may soon force you to confront reality could be the gateway to your greatest personal and perhaps mutual achievement.

Card seventeen means: the stronger your Faith in a higher power the easier Hope can refresh and rejuvenate your life now.

At your best, your best "luck" stems from your willingness to heed sound advice and follow your own higher instincts. At work and home your calm and rational approach helps everyone retain their focus upon the matter at hand.

Under more stressful conditions however, since you're as emotional as you are intuitive, an overabundance of any emotion can cause you to misinterpret your intuition.

Card 18 The Moon

The more constructively you channel your emotions the better all your endeavors will fare. Caution.

Your desire for self-achievement and recognition is equally balanced against your desire to help and be helped by others. The delicate balance between your emotional perspective, material assets and opportunities is subject to change without notice. If you are feeling melancholy, irritable, suspicious or anxious and unable to pinpoint the exact source of your distress, you may soon hear several pieces of bad news from or about people you know and care for. If you cannot and have not been able to shake your melancholy now is a good time to consult with a professional counselor or religious advisor. The more constructively you channel your emotions, the better all your endeavors will fare. Physically, you're more susceptible to nervous upsets and ailments that can be a by product of stress. Emotionally, the more you feel you need to be needed to feel good about you, the more vulnerable you are to slights and criticisms. Some of your relationships may even take on new depth and meaning once you realize you don't need them in order to exist. Your emotions are restless. Your intuition is keen.

The more encouraging the other cards in the spread, the easier you can relax by doing things you enjoy. This will allow solutions to your problems to come to you and prevent you from taking out your frustrations on others or yourself.

The more challenging the situation or the other cards in the spread the more likely you are entrenching yourself in denial, about your job, health or relationships. This self-defeating cycle aligns your energy, fears and anger against each opportunity you have to change things for the better.

Key word:

Caution

Card18
The Moon

Tip:
If this card appears in reverse (or upside-down) Whatever your situation, any matters you may have been hiding (or hiding from) as well as some that have been hidden from you are more likely to be revealed.

Card eighteen means: the necessity of looking at matters more closely now. Being honest with yourself as well as others really is the best policy now.

At your best, by working with whatever new facts "come to light" now, you can be particularly innovative concerning matters from finance to romance and everything in between.

Under more stressful conditions however, you can become overwhelmed by emotional or material preoccupations that will prove counterproductive to what you hope to achieve.

Card 19 The Sun

Success can be yours by expending the right balance of energy, ambition, and emotion. Personal Enlightenment.

Your ambitions are like Pandora's box. The effort you expend to achieve them will unleash greater challenges and opportunities than you expect. Success can be yours, no matter what the challenge by expending the right balance of energy, ambition, and emotion. Taking the time to combine your willpower with patience will enhance your creativity and resourcefulness enabling you to easily move mountains. The manner in which you respond to others now, will begin to reveal each person or situation's purpose in your life and your purpose related to them – like the rising sun.

The more encouraging the other cards in the spread, the easier you can attract and influence other people. This is a time for sharing and receiving good news, from job to romance, pregnancy and everything in between. In tense moments adopting a non-judgmental manner can help everyone relax while enabling you to get great results from even the most difficult people. You can count on a resourceful network of friends and acquaintances to provide you with good connections and information.

The more challenging the situation or the other cards in the spread, the more you can count on some type of bright spot to see you through matters even if you are (or have been) courting physical, emotional or professional burn-out. Frustration with what you consider to be the worst in matters now, can be the catalyst that brings out the best in you. Don't allow your stronger brighter self to be eclipsed by self-doubt or trying to impress or save the people and situations that are wrong for you.

Key word:

Enlightenment

Card 19

The Sun

Tip:

If this card appears in re-verse (or upside-down) whether you're expecting too much, too soon or whether you're simply trying too hard in matters now, the possibility of you experiencing some type of personal burn-out in the near future is higher than usual.

Card nineteen means: whatever the situation you are likely to feel quite optimistic or view matters in a more positive light.

At your best, the more comfortable you are with yourself now the less likely you are to encounter any serious friction in your relationships at work, home or both!

Under more stressful conditions however, a Narcissistic tem-perament coupled with a bad temper can emerge.

Card 20 Judgment

Certain issues that you thought you'd resolved, as well as some you've been avoiding, will be resurfacing. Revelation.

The more you think you know what you're going to do and where you're going now in matters, the more likely you'll soon change your mind and direction. The more you absorb and work with truths you cannot escape, the more improvement you will see. Whether these issues concern your perspective, your feelings, your health, your goals, your job or your relationships, something will force you to make decisions or face facts you'd rather avoid. Just remember that no matter how inconvenient their arrival, whatever new facts, developments or information you receive can also prove to be blessings in disguise – whether by offering you a chance to make your best even better or preventing you from making an even bigger mistake.

The more encouraging the other cards in the spread, the easier it will be for you to resolve matters and clear the air without incurring additional misconceptions. You may soon receive some type of vindication or exoneration or even the means to transform what appears to be a disaster into an absolute success.

The more challenging the situation or the other cards in the spread the longer it may take to resolve matters. However, until you do resolve matters your endeavors will remain in limbo or out-of-step. You may feel that tying-up-the-loose-ends, is the story of your life. Whether you seem to keep starting over from the bottom of the ladder or a little closer to the top, depends upon whether you're really learning what you need to know. Procrastination, rather than bad luck, may be your biggest enemy.

Key word:

Revelation

Card 20

Judgment

Tip:

If this card appears in reverse (or upside-down) whatever your situation putting some distance between your emotions and the facts could improve your judgment and prevent you from making the wrong choice or move.

Card twenty means: questioning the wisdom of continuing or beginning a certain course of action or behavior.

At your best, the more in tune you are with yourself the easier you can rely on your own logic and rationality to arrive at the best decisions – despite outside pressure from others' opinions and suggestions.

Under more stressful conditions however, you may be too quick to notice and blame other people's mistakes without ever recognizing your own.

Card 21 The World

Fresh starts and second chances that you make, as well as those which are offered to you. Freedom.

The less willing you are to free yourself from bad habits or emotional dependencies, the less good they will do you. The World celebrates forgiveness. How to forgive others, how to accept forgiveness and (most importantly) how to forgive yourself so that you can make the fresh start that leads to a happy ending. At this time, giving yourself something positive to look forward and setting goals that are more realistic than idealistic can make you feel more alive than anything else can. Since your freedom to act and react as you see fit are especially precious to you now, this is an ideal time for starting anything new from an attitude, to a diet and exercise program, to job or relationship and everything in between.

The more encouraging the other cards in the spread, the easier it will be for you to uphold your new resolutions and enjoy life. The better you feel about yourself and whatever you're doing the easier you can coerce your opponents and achieve your own ends more peacefully. You can coax opportunity to come to you now, simply by being yourself. At work and home, in many larger and smaller instances you can emerge as a leader now, setting the pace and blazing new trails. Medically and even legally, you just might move mountains now.

The more challenging the situation or the other cards in the spread the more challenging it will be to use the pressure you're under to launch yourself in a better direction instead of falling back into the same old rut. Everything that you fail to start for the right reasons will never become what you envision – no matter how hard you try.

Key word:

Freedom

Card 21

The World

Tip:

If this card appears in reverse (or upside-down) beware the temptation to overextend your budget and overstep emotionally boundaries.

Card twenty-one means: fresh starts and second chances.

At your best, whatever your situation, your needs and interests are expanding at a faster pace, enabling you to be more of a self-starter than usual, or ever before. One or more fortunate business, social or romantic connections or opportunities may even come your way like magic!

Under more stressful conditions however, whatever the situation you may become too daring, or devious in ways that can make others uneasy.

Card 22 The Fool

You are about to embark upon a new chapter in your life. Motivation.

If you remember that nothing in life is fool-proof, you won't lose your balance between reality and fantasy. Consciously, subconsciously, or both, you're ready and willing to take more responsibility for your own success and happiness. You are about to embark upon a new chapter in your life and you are cautiously optimistic. Whether you're about to begin or seek a new job, make a change in residence (or changes within your residence), begin or end a course of study – or a relationship, you're going to experience new (or renewed) self-confidence. You're relying on you more than ever to make your dreams come true. You may be traveling more or meeting new people in the near future.

The more encouraging the other cards in the spread, the easier you can put your new plans in motion. This is a marvelous time to cultivate introductions and establish or renew acquaintanceships with people whose professional or even political standing might open some doors for you. Professionally and financially, the greater your determination to succeed the sooner your focus will shift from merely gratifying your immediate desires to perfecting your talents and creating your own opportunities. If you're in the market for romance treating yourself to a vacation or changing your social habits in the near future could be the catalyst that sets your social life or love-life back on track.

The more challenging the situation or the other cards in the spread the more likely you may be fooling yourself again, or simply trying to impress or save the wrong people.

Key word:

Motivation

Card 22

The Fool

Tip:

If this card appears in reverse (or upside-down) whatever your situation, beware impatience and over optimism.

Card twenty-two means: you can be a true visionary now. The more headway you see you are making in matters, the more you stand to gain by practicing cautious expansion.

At your best, you can immerse yourself in every aspect of whatever you are doing. At work and home, you are uncommonly resourceful and patient in your quest to achieve the best results.

Under more stressful conditions however, your quest for personal gain or achievement may cause you to lose touch with reality, as well as the needs and feelings of other people. Too late you may realize that you're living in a fools paradise.

CHAPTER 2

Court and Subject Cards

The Minor Arcana

Minor Arcana Cards tell the story behind the Major Arcana's headlines.

The Minor Arcana outlines the events surrounding the karmic situations that were suggested by the Major Arcana. The Minor Arcana contain 56 cards and its name translates into "Small Secrets." Collectively as well as individually, Minor Arcana cards reveal matters that are or will be happening now. If you are planning to attend a party Saturday night you may not feel impressed if your reader mentions it. Yet, the fact that it was mentioned means that attending that party will prove more significant than you are aware. Why? Because you're going to have more or less fun than you expected whether or not the reader provides specific details. Elsewhere in the reading, you may hear you'll soon meet someone new or be "under the weather". You could meet that "someone new" after the party or through another party guest. You might contract a cold or the flu from someone else that attended the party. Readings are like life — it's the smaller episodes that make the biggest differences!

The Minor Arcana contains four suits of cards. Each suit consists of 14 cards, and it's interesting to note that the keyword for Card or Number 14 is Compromise. Each suit relates to one of the four elements: Fire, Air, Water and Earth. We will address them in the following chapters.

The following information will be particularly helpful for anyone with a desire to work more closely with the Tarot. However, it can prove to be an invaluable asset in bringing to life any of the many exquisite 78 card Tarot Decks whose Minor Arcana Subject Cards (two through ten) feature symbols (such as four cups floating in the air) instead of pictures.

Court Cards and Subject Cards

The Court Cards

The first five cards in each suit are the King, Queen, Knight, Page and Ace. Collectively, they are known as the Court Cards. The more Court Cards there are in your reading, the more interaction you will have (for better or worse) with or because of a situation related to influential people, older people or authority figures at work, home or both. Planning a wedding, or preparing to interview for a new job – even making plans to relocate are more pleasant examples. Planning legal strategies, or working to restore peace whether between yourself and a friend or within your family are less pleasant, but applicable examples.

ALL Kings Trigger or Enhance Your Personal Initiative

Above all the element (Air, Earth, Fire or Water) that rules each King enhances your personal initiative and lends you a specific behavioral advantage that can provide the upper hand you need to achieve a goal or mount a solid defense. Although each King can sometimes signify a job promotion, demotion or a change in duties or announce the entrance of a new man with the potential to change your life in some capacity, they **always** enhance your personal initiative and leadership whether to set new wheels in motion or handle any situation more effectively. The more encouraging the other cards in the spread, the more strategic your maneuvers and methods will be. The more challenging the other cards in the spread, the less self-control you may exert – acting and reacting without consideration or regard for the consequences. The more Kings there are in the spread the more important your relationships with men or authority figures may be to your progress, but regardless, your behavior will need to be modified and diversified. In addition to the basic keyword that describes their suit, each King also shares the keyword Initiative. The King of Wands = Changeable/ Initiative. King of Cups = Emotional/Initiative. King of Swords = Challenging/Initiative. King of Pentacles = Ambitious/Initiative.

ALL Queens display a particular charisma that can enhance your personal coping skills.

Above all, the element (Air, Earth, Fire or Water) that rules each Queen strengthens your ability to make the most or best of matters and situations, by lending you a charismatic appeal that can charm, coerce or reveal your detractors. Though not as often as Kings, each Queens can sometimes signify a job promotion, demotion or a change in duties, or announce the entrance of a new woman with the potential to change your life in some capacity. More than anything else however, Queens represent to your ability and desire to keep everyone and everything on "the same page" by managing matters and people at home, work or both more effectively. The more encouraging the other cards in the spread, the more often your influence will provide a positive source of inspiration upon everything and everyone around you. The more challenging the other cards in the spread, the more likely you are to instigate chaos to get your own way in matters. The more Queens there are in the spread, the more important your associations with women may be to your progress but regardless, your coping skills will need to be especially flexible. In addition to the basic keyword that describes their suit each Queen also shares the keyword Charisma. The Queen of Wands = Changeable / Charisma. Queen of Cups = Emotional/Charisma. Queen of Swords = Challenging / Charisma. Queen of Pentacles = Ambitious / Charisma.

Knights are Reactionaries. ALL Knights indicate sudden developments in matters or your behavior.

The best or worst of the Knight's energy is set in motion by your perception of people and matters that stand between you and what you're hoping to accomplish. The more encouraging the other cards in the spread, the more quickly and effectively you can deal with new developments as they arise. The more challenging the other cards in the spread, the harder you may have to work to stay on top of matters or defend your position. The more Knights there are in the spread, the more you can expect your plans to be interrupted by a combination of pleasant and annoying interludes. In addition to the basic keyword that describes their suit each Knight also shares the keyword Adventure. The Knight of Wands = Changeable/ Adventure. Knight of Cups = Emotional/Adventure. Knight of Swords = Challenging/Adventure. Knight of Pentacles = Ambitious/Adventure.

ALL Pages signals small matters with the potential to grow larger.

A Page sometimes indicates children, grandchildren or pregnancy. In general however, the more encouraging the other cards in the spread, the more likely you are to make the most of small surprises, opportunities and ideas that can make big differences. The more challenging the other cards in the spread, the more likely you are to make mountains out of molehills. The more Pages in the spread, the more and different types of news, information and gossip you can expect to receive. However, check your sources before you pass along any secrets or rumors that you hear. In addition to the basic keyword that describes their suit each Page also shares the keyword Surprises. The Page of Wands = Changeable/ Surprises. Knight of Cups = Emotional/Surprises. Knight of Swords = Challenging/Surprises. Page of Pentacles = Ambitious/Surprises.

ALL Aces Signify an Outcome - a Crisis or Reward.

Each Ace indicates that an inevitable showdown is approaching, whether with yourself, matters or other people. The more encouraging the other cards in the spread, the closer you will come to achieving a goal you've been working towards. The more challenging the other cards in the spread, the more critical matters will prove to be. An Ace indicates a major – sometimes unique turning point in your life that can accompany triumph or tragedy. The more Aces there are in the spread, the more you stand to gain or lose through your behavior. Each Ace is accompanied by only the Keywords Crisis/Reward .

The Subject Cards

Cards Two (2) through Ten (10) in each Suit of the Minor Arcana Tarot Cards are known as the Subject Cards. Though not as dramatic as the Court Cards, Subject Cards wield a power all their own. Working with the subject at hand to produce a successful conclusion is what life is all about. Getting the best out of a subject without allowing it to get the better of you is an art! Successfully changing a subject, no matter how redundant or pointless it has become, is always more difficult than giving way to self-pity or submitting to its unreasonable demands. Here is a complete list of all the subject cards in each suit.

Wands Subject Cards

Card 28 Two of Wands is the 2nd of the Wands subject cards.

Card 29 Three of Wands is the 3rd of the Wands subject cards.

Card 30 Four of Wands is the 4th of the Wands subject cards.

Card 31 Five of Wands is the 5th of the Wands subject cards.

Card 32 Six of Wands is the 6th of the Wands subject cards.

Card 33 Seven of Wands is the 7th of the Wands subject cards.

Card 34 Eight of Wands is the 8th of the Wands subject cards.

Card 35 Nine of Wands is the 9th of the Wands subject cards.

Card 36 Ten of Wands is the 10th and last of the Wands subject cards.

Cups

Card 42 Two of Cups is the 2nd of the Cups subject cards.

Card 43 Three of Cups is the 3rd of the Cups subject cards.

Card 44 Four of Cups is the 4th of the Cups subject cards.

Card 45 Five of cups is the 5th of the Cups subject cards.

Card 46 Six of Cups is the 6th of the Cups subject cards.

Card 47 Seven of Cups is the 7th of the Cups subject cards.

Card 48 Eight of Cups is the 8th of the Cups subject cards.

Card 49 Nine of Cups is the 9th of the Cups subject cards.

Card 50 Ten of Cups is the 10th and last of the Cups subject cards.

Swords

Card 51 Two of Swords is the 2nd of the Swords subject cards

Card 52 Three of Swords is the 3rd of the Swords subject cards

Card 53 Four of Swords is the 4th of the Swords subject cards

Card 54 Five of Swords is the 5th of the Swords subject cards

Card 55 Six of Swords is the 6th of the Swords subject cards

Card 56 Seven of Swords is the 7th of the Swords subject cards

Card 57 Eight of Swords is the 8th of the Sword subject cards

Card 58 Nine of Swords is the 9th of the Sword subject cards

Card 59 Ten of Swords is the 10th of the Swords subject cards

Pentacles

Card 70 Two of Pentacles is the 2nd of the Pentacles subject cards.

Card 71 Three of Pentacles is the 3rd of the Pentacles subject cards.

Card 72 Four of Pentacles is the 4th of the Pentacles subject cards.

Card 73 Five of Pentacles is the 5th of the Pentacles subject cards.

Card 74 Six of Pentacles is the 6th of the Pentacles subject cards.

Card 75 Seven of Pentacles is the 7th of the Pentacles subject cards.

Card 76 Eight of Pentacles is the 8th of the Pentacles subject cards.

Card 77 Nine of Pentacles is the 9th of the Pentacles subject cards.

Card 78 Ten of Pentacles is the 10th and last of the Pentacles subject cards.

Here are basic guidelines for beginning your interpretation of each Subject Card from any one of the four (4) suits in the Minor Arcana. Beginning on Page 91 in Chapter 3 you will discover that each subject card is accompanied by the basic keyword that describes it's function as well as one more keyword that suggests its behavior according to its Suit as a handy means of reminding and reinforcing what you've learned. For example, on Page91 the Two of Wands reads Challenging/Interaction. Card 42 The Two of Cups reads Emotional/Interaction. Card 56 The Two of Swords reads Challenging/Interaction and Card 70 The Two of Pentacles reads Ambitious/Interaction.

Subject card number 2 represents INTERACTION.

The second subject card outlines your level of passion and determination to achieve and maintain your emotional and material goals. When the number "2" repeats itself in a reading, you may need to consult more people than you expected or more people than usual may request favors or advice from you. Despite it's fondness for company, the 2nd subject card also contains a strong element of self-interest and self-preservation. The Element (Air, Earth, Fire or Water) that rules the Tarot Card will indicate whether you'll find it a little easier or more challenging to interact constructively with other people. The more encouraging the other cards in the spread, the easier you can gain whatever assistance, approval or co-operation you may require. The more challenging the other cards in the spread, the more resistance or delays you are likely to encounter.

Subject card number 3 represents THINKING and NETWORKING.

The third subject card describes how you absorb and react to whatever is happening around you at home and at work—from get-togethers to emergencies. It pertains to your ability and desire to rationalize matters. The Element (Air, Earth, Fire or Water) that rules the Tarot Card indicates whether your manner of self-expression is likely to benefit or harm your communication. The more threes there are in your reading, the more your success will depend upon your desire or refusal to "think before you react" to what you hear. The more encouraging the other cards in the spread, the more rewarding and, perhaps, revealing your communications will be. You'll find it easier to meet your obligations and tackle any emergencies that arise. The more challenging the other cards in the spread, the more resistance or delays you may encounter in traveling as well as delivering and interpreting ideas and messages.

Subject card number 4 represents INCENTIVE and SECURITY.

The fourth subject card corresponds to your methods of control and handling of anyone or anything that impacts your sense of security and belonging at work, home or both. It suggests your incentive for beginning, completing or quitting matters. The Element (Air, Earth, Fire or Water) that rules the Tarot Card indicates whether you're really ready to launch new projects or looking for someplace to hide from matters you aren't ready to confront. Anytime the number four repeats itself in a reading, for whatever reason, your peace of mind will soon be called into question. The more encouraging the other cards in the spread, the easier you could complete matters to your satisfaction and everyone's best interest. The more challenging the other cards in the spread, the longer you may procrastinate or the more resistance or delays you may encounter.

Subject card number 5 represents CONFLICTS.

Since the fifth subject card represents your desire to be noticed, loved and above all, appreciated, it also signals an on-going struggle between the higher and lower elements in your nature. The Element (Air, Earth, Fire or Water) that rules the Tarot

Card indicates whether your efforts to get your way in matters will prove more rewarding or exasperating. The fifth subject card of any suit tends to trigger some type of conflict – whether between your logic and your emotions or yourself and other people. The more 'fives" you find throughout your reading, the more your will power, creativity and flexibility is likely to be tested by matters and other people. The more encouraging the other cards in the spread, the easier it will be to bring forth the best in you and your endeavors by applying constructive self-control and self-discipline. The more challenging the other cards in the spread, the harder you may make matters on yourself due to self-doubt or indecision.

Subject card number 6 represents <u>YOUR LEVEL OF COMMITMENT.</u>

The sixth subject card deals with your general health, your daily routine and your willingness to make whatever changes may be necessary to keep matters running more smoothly, efficiently and harmoniously. The Element (Air, Earth, Fire or Water) that rules the Tarot Card indicates whether it will be easier or more challenging to commit your energies to constructive endeavors. Anytime more than one "six" appears in your reading, the busier your schedule will be. The more encouraging the other cards in the spread, the easier you can attain and maintain a constructive focus and routine. The more challenging the other cards in the spread, (for whatever reason) you are likely to encounter a little more resistance or delays in accomplishing your daily routine.

Subject card number 7 represents <u>your</u> <u>PERSONAL</u> and <u>PROFESSIONAL</u> <u>ASSOCIATIONS.</u>

The seventh subject card represents the constructive or self-destructive manner in which you are handling all your relationships. The Element (Air, Earth, Fire or Water) that rules the Tarot Card indicates whether now is your time to shine or revise your strategy. Should you notice more than one "7" in your reading, you'd be wise to take less for granted now in any of your relationships. The more encouraging the other cards in the spread, the easier and farther your people skills can take you. The more challenging the other cards in the spread, the more resistance or delays you are likely to encounter in your relationships.

Subject card number 8 is a card for RENOVATION.

The eighth subject card is primarily concerned with your future due to the choices you've made in the past. It offers clues about your future with anything or anyone that is valuable to you. For example, the stability of your relationships and your source of income, as well as your health and the health or prosperity of those you care for. The Element (Air, Earth, Fire or Water) that rules the Tarot Card indicates whether it will be a little easier or more challenging to preserve or improve matters. The more "eights" you see throughout your reading, the more work you have ahead of you. The more encouraging the other cards in the spread, the easier and more enjoyable your work will be. The more challenging the other cards in the spread, the more resistance or delays you are likely to encounter until you readjust your focus or priorities and possibly both.

Subject card number 9 represents_your UNDERSTANDING.

The ninth subject card tests your beliefs , goals, values and understanding. Whenever it's repeated in a reading, you may need to re-examine certain aspects of yourself, matters and other people. The Element (Air, Earth, Fire or Water) that rules the Tarot Card indicates whether it will be easier or more challenging to expand your outlook for the betterment of matters. The more encouraging the other cards in the spread, the easier it will be to reach a better understanding of yourself and other people. The more challenging the other cards in the spread, the more complications and contradictions you may have to unravel to achieve a better understanding.

Subject card number 10 represents ACHIEVEMENT.

The 10th and last subject card can be a mixed blessing. It will sometimes reveal a reward for your recent efforts or a lesson you have mastered. However, it can sometimes reveal a complication or delay that is standing in the way of your achievement. The tenth and last subject card represents rewards and penalties. Whether or not you've chosen to make the most of your opportunities, anytime the 10th subject card appears more than once in a reading, it can generate a great deal of "instant karma" that can suddenly change the course of matters, for better or worse, through your behavior and attitude. The Element (Air, Earth, Fire or Water) that rules the Tarot Card indicates the manner in which you could create or cost yourself the outcome you desire. The more encouraging the other cards in the spread, the easier you can adjust your attitude and behavior to insure the outcome you desire. The more challenging the other cards in the spread, whether or not you like the outcomes that you devise, will be secondary to your willingness to deal with them constructively.

CHAPTER 3

Wands

The Wands - Change

Keyword: <u>Change</u>   Element: <u>Fire</u>

Corresponding Astrological Signs: Aries ♈, Leo ♌, and Sagittarius ♐

Corresponding Playing Card: Diamonds.

Wands indicate the type of impact that the changes you make and encounter will have upon matters

Like the Fire Signs, Wands blaze their own trail. Wands imply Change that can lead to personal renewal. Wands can help us accept the necessity of making some changes and adapt to others.

Wands represent spontaneity, sudden gains, and opportunity — or opposition — that may come out of nowhere. The more encouraging the situation or other cards in the spread, the easier and more quickly you can make certain changes and prevent others from unbalancing your agenda. The more challenging the situation or other cards in the spread the less likely you are to make all the changes you'd hoped to and the more you need to beware of depleting your energy and encountering personal burn out. If the majority of the spread consists of Wands, it will be more challenging to pronounce a definite outcome. You are about to encounter a very active and possibly adventurous or somewhat annoying time period. Your need to accommodate incoming changes, at home, at work, or both, may limit the number of changes you can make. Resist the temptation to let your temper get the better of you; the more willing you are to work with matters, the more you will benefit later from everything you do and learn now.

Card 23 The King of Wands

Kings can trigger or enhance your personal initiative.

Good or bad, the King of Wands makes his own luck and so can you! Material ease, or professional acclaim, as well as emotional happiness can be yours – though they may not manifest in the time or manner that you expect.

The more encouraging the situation or other cards in the spread, the more energetically and enthusiastically you will approach each task and/or dilemma you encounter. At work and home, your ability to take charge of matters, and complete them in less time than you expected, may even surprise you! Your sense of humor is the perfect complement and companion for your self-assertion, enabling you to impress and convince other people effortlessly. Meetings or interviews with authority figures are likely to go better than you'd hoped.

The more challenging the situation or other cards in the spread the harder it may be for you to control matters or your temper. Meetings or interviews with authority figures are likely to prove counterproductive. You will begin more matters (and possibly more disagreements) than you can or really care to complete. You may make impulsive changes that you could regret later.

Romantically: Should your spread contain a hint of romance, you may suddenly develop an attraction for someone you've just met or known for awhile and go out of your way to gain their attention – perhaps without realizing it.

The more reassuring the other cards, the key ingredient to a lasting relationship may be the ease with which you can accept and respect the differences in each other's personalities.

The less reassuring the other cards, the more likely your attraction (or relationship) will burn itself (and you) out.

Key word:

Changeable Initiative

Card 23

The King of Wands, Rods, Staves

Tip:

If this card appears in reverse (or upside-down) it signifies initiative that may be misdirected

RE DI BASTONI
ROI DE BATONS

KING OF WANDS
REY DE BASTOS

KÖNIG DER STÄBE

STAVEN KONING

Card twenty-three means: although you can be more impatient than you appear, you are also particularly resourceful when you're under pressure.

At your best, you earn other people's respect and affection in a manner that is as positive as it is productive. You work for the joy of doing, and your time is well-structured whether you are putting a new project together or dashing to attend a class.

Under more stressful conditions however, the easier other people try to make matters for you the harder you make matters for yourself. In an instant your moods can become too intense, dramatic or extreme, causing you to embarrass yourself and others.

Card 24 The Queen of Wands

Queens can enhance your charisma and people skills.

Professionally and materially the fact that you can be an excellent judge of other people's potential and character is generally accompanied by a knack for steering matters and opinion in your favor. However, your attraction to and for people who inspire your imagination, and curiosity can sometimes invite more intrigue than adventure into your personal realm.

The more encouraging the situation or other cards in the spread, the easier you can enlist other people's co-operation and charm their sensibilities by your positive example. At work and at home, you will encounter less opposition concerning even the most radical changes you make. This is an excellent time to gain an introduction to people who can further your interests. You may even negotiate a successful truce between opposing factions at work, at home, or both.

The more challenging the situation or other cards in the spread the less charming you will feel and appear. The harder you try to mask your anxiety or irritability, the more obvious and contagious it becomes. You could start trouble between other people without being aware of it.

Romantically: Should your spread contain a hint of romance, whether or not you're aware of it, your desire to be noticed and appreciated will increase – enhancing your romantic powers of attraction.

The more reassuring the other cards, the more likely you are to attract a wide variety of suitors whose goals and personalities complement your need for change, sense of adventure or both.

The less reassuring the other cards, the more likely you are to make a nuisance of yourself, alienating not only the object of your affection, but possibly a friend or two as well.

Key words:

Changeable/ Charisma

Card 24

The Queen of Wands, Rods, Staves

Tip:

If this card appears in reverse (or upside-down) it signifies charisma that may attract the wrong elements

REGINA DI BASTONI   QUEEN OF WANDS
REINE DE BATONS   REINA DE BASTOS

KÖNIGIN DER STÄBE   STAVEN KONINGIN

Card twenty-four means: Your people skills are one of your greatest keys to success.

At your best, your enthusiasm is as charismatic as your confidence, and your keen powers of visualization can enable you to work wonders!

Under more stressful conditions however, the close link between your emotions and your pride can interfere with your objectivity and wreak havoc in all areas of your life.

Card 25 the Knight of Wands

Knights indicate unexpected developments in matters or your behavior.

Each Knight has the potential to trigger a different type of behavior. The Knight of Wands enables you to meet unexpected changes more resourcefully.

The more encouraging the situation or other cards in the spread, the easier you can turn any potential disadvantage into an advantage. At work or home, you will be less reluctant to adopt the attitude you need to accomplish things properly. Your flexibility and spontaneity may even surprise you! At work and home, you will discover more options and choices than you expected.

The more challenging the situation or other cards in the spread, the more your patience will be tried by petty annoyances, interruptions and other people's lack of consideration at work and at home. You may waste more time or money than you'd intended or more than you can afford on a matter. Events may force you to speak up for yourself – which could help clear the air or earn you respect – but only if you watch what you say and how you say it. Try to be more careful when traveling too; allow yourself extra time to reach your destination.

Romantically: Should your spread contain a hint of romance, the more likely you are to suddenly begin or end a romantic pursuit or relationship.

The more reassuring the situation or other cards in the spread, the more likely you are to accept a date with someone whether or not you'd been hoping they'd ask. You may even surprise yourself by making the first move! You could suddenly decide to become a couple with a current – or previous date-mate.

The less reassuring the situation or other cards in the spread, the more tempting it may be to take a romantic risk that you will regret sooner than you think.

Keywords:

Changeable Adventure

Card 25

The Knight of Wands, Rods, Staves

Tip:

If this card appears in reverse (or upside-down) it signifies adventure but it may bring more than you bargained for.

Card twenty-five means: You need to be more observant of what's happening around you now. Stay flexible.

At your best, you can "go with the flow" when prudent and swim confidently against the prevailing current when necessary to reach your goals. "Can-Do", is your motto!

Under more stressful conditions however, you may treat life with too much contempt, or always have to be the center of attention.

Card 26 the Page of Wands

Pages signal small matters with the potential to grow larger.

The more encouraging the situation or other cards in the spread, the easier you will notice and take small opportunities to blaze your own trail in matters at work and at home. You're likely to receive several small but welcome pieces of good news, invitations or welcome interruptions in your daily routine. This could be the ideal time to take or plan a small "getaway". Should unexpected company arrive, hosting or entertaining them will be more of a pleasure than an ordeal.

The more challenging the situation or other cards in the spread, the harder it may be for you to resist taking petty advantage. A number of last-minute changes from other people could upset your agenda. Page Cards sometimes provide a message concerning children, or grandchildren under the age of 25. As a rule, **the more favorable** the surrounding cards the lighter the message – perhaps an opportunity to travel. **The less favorable** the surrounding cards the more likely a matter relating to the young persons family life or their companions could trigger small changes in their behavior that may become a source of ongoing concern.

Romantically: Should your spread contain a hint of romance, small changes that could make big differences may be on the horizon in your current relationship or social attitude and environment!

The more reassuring the other cards in the spread, accepting an invitation to take a short trip or attend a small gathering could lead to the discovery that your social skills and power of attraction aren't as rusty as you imagined!

The less reassuring the other cards in the spread, the more you may feel your relationship is changing in small ways that are making you uncomfortable and you are at a loss to explain.

Keywords:

Changeable Surprises

Card 26

The Page of Wands, Rods, Staves

Tip:

If this card appears in reverse (or upside-down) it may signify series of small surprises containing a mixture of good and bad news

FANTE DI BASTONI
VALET DE BATONS

KNAVE OF WANDS
SOTA DE BASTOS

BUBE DER STÄBE   STAVEN SCHILDKNAAP

Card twenty-six means: small changes (in yourself, matters and people) that can make big differences are on the horizon.

At your best, you can be child-like without being childish. You can always discover something to look forward to.

Under more stressful conditions however, whatever the cause you may have to work a little harder than you expected to reach your professional or academic goals. Instead of "child-like" you may become childish, selfish, and manipulative.

27 the Ace of Wands

Aces represent crisis or reward.

The more encouraging the situation or other cards in the spread, the more pleased you'll be by a new turn of events at work or at home. You stand to benefit greatly, whether in the near future or the long run, from changes that begin now even if you are not causing them to happen. Whether you will be offered the opportunity or be forced to make changes in your job, attitude, or behavior, you'll be glad you did. Dramatic changes that might occur in the company you work for could result in a promotion for you or cause you to make a happier and more lucrative job change.

The more challenging the situation or other cards in the spread, the greater the risk of burning yourself out to no avail by trying to force matters to go your way.

Romantically: Should your spread contain a hint of romance, whether or not you are romantically involved, dramatic changes, in your self-awareness will trigger changes in your **emotional habits and behavior.**

The more reassuring the other cards in the spread, an increase in your financial security could revive your desire for companionship, or enable you and your loved one to begin making the best aspects of your relationship even better.

The less reassuring the other cards in the spread, your relationship may prove more vulnerable than you expected to outside pressures from other people's problems. You may surprise others (as well as yourself) by beginning a relationship that you know is doomed to fail. You or your loved one may suddenly decide to end your relationship at a time or in a manner that takes you both by surprise.

Keywords:

Crisis/Reward

Card 27

The Ace of Wands, Rods, Staves

Tip:

If this card appears in reverse (or upside-down) it may signify the approach of major changes due to matters beyond your control.

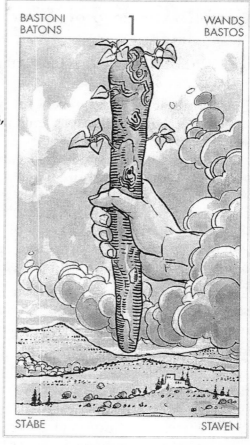

Card twenty-seven means: Major Changes.Circumstance as well as your personal aspirations will force you to blaze your own trail through matters in ways and at times when you least expect it.

At your best, When, you choose to harness your willpower with a positive attitude, success can be yours in any area. Just remember that with any Ace halfway measures, attitudes and solutions will not be good enough.

Under more stressful conditions however, if you are unwilling to take responsibility for your mistakes you could seriously undermine your progress.

Card 28 the Two of Wands

Subject Card Two signifies interaction.

Events that take place at work, at home, or both, will present you with the opportunity to make some changes you'd like to see. Since your instincts for self-preservation are just as strong as your desire to blaze your own trail the wonders that you can accomplish under pressure may surprise you as much as they amaze others, you have the ability to transform dreams into reality. Humility, hard work, humor and honesty are your keys to professional happiness, peace of mind and accomplishment. Any time your ego encourages you to climb too high, you'll experience a painful fall back into reality.

Emotionally, the longer it takes for you to develop the necessary patience for untangling fantasy from fact, the longer it may take before you find the personal happiness you deserve.

The more encouraging the situation or other cards in the spread, the more you will have only yourself to thank or blame for changes that you make or refuse to make. Here comes your opening, complete with other people's good will, to prove a point, receive vindication or extricate yourself gracefully from a matter, job or relationship. Your uncanny ability to separate your feelings from the fact in matters can help you make even the most challenging choices and decisions more easily now.

The more challenging the situation or other cards in the spread the more you may procrastinate about taking advantage of an opportunity either because you doubt your abilities or you encounter more resistance than support from other people. Indecision may cause you to be susceptible to intimidation or manipulation from other people, making it more likely that you will regret not having trusted your own instincts and followed your original plan.

Key words:

Changeable/ Interaction

Card 28

The Two of Wands, Rods, Staves

Tip:

If this card appears in re-verse (or upside-down) you would be wise to take the time you need to get your facts straight before making a deci-sion or a fuss now.

Card twenty-eight means: You need to be a more realistic than idealistic now.

At your best, your ability to remain focused helps you remain calm and aware of, as well as open to, many solutions, oppor-tunities and ideas other people may miss or ignore.

Under more stressful conditions however, you may be too quick to involve yourself and others in idealistic schemes based on assumption rather than fact.

Card 29 the Three of Wands

Subject Card Three is for thinking and networking.

At this time, you could overcome incredible odds (even emotional or psychological shackles) to reach a particular goal that you may decide was your destiny. Who can say it wasn't? Events at work and home will provide unexpected opportunities for you. You may be able to impart helpful suggestions and ideas that could save the day and bring you positive recognition. At work, home or both -you may be the first person to receive some type of significant news. Personally, professionally (or both) the stronger your ambition the more likely you will notice an increase in your social and professional opportunities. Your ability to communicate effectively with others on a professional or material level may be more in evidence. In personal settings, however, unless you choose your words carefully now, you may create more misunderstandings than you resolve.

The more encouraging the situation or other cards in the spread, the easier it will be for you say the right thing or provide the correct answer. You are particularly resourceful now – ready and able to accommodate last-minute changes in your own and other people's agendas. You may launch a new idea, concept or theory that will benefit others and enrich your bank account.

The more challenging the situation or other cards in the spread, the more likely you or someone else may let the other down at the last minute, by changing your story or withholding information. You cannot afford to count on last-minute rescues or reprieves. The majority of your actions and decisions need to be based on a "do-it-yourself" attitude that will encourage self-reliance.

Keyword:

Changeable/Thinking, Networking

Card 29

The Three of Wands, Rods, Staves

Tip:

If this card appears in reverse (or upside-down) it still signifies discovery, but part of what you discover may be a fresh obstacle or delay.

Card twenty-nine means: The greater your concern or anticipation about the future the more you need to concentrate on handling your current responsibilities and obligations.

At your best, you can easily alternate between being giving and following orders, depending on which role is more important to your success.

Under more stressful conditions however, your talent for making others believe what you say, or your ability to disguise your short-comings may fail you.

Card 30 the Four of Wands

Subject Card Four stands for incentive and security.

Events at work and home will provide unexpected opportunities for you make changes. These changes can reinforce your security, bring additional moral support or encouragement that could motivate you – if motivation has been a problem for you. Whatever your situation or concern, from finance to romance, (and everything in between) the Four of Wands can be one of the most fortunate cards in the Tarot. Since you can master the basics in matters and other people more quickly now, some folks will also be more receptive to whatever explanations, apologies or advice you might offer. Just beware of becoming too sure of yourself or taking advantage of situations and other people. Promising more today, than you can deliver in the future, as well as hearing and seeing only what you want to in matters now, can be a downside to the Four of Wands.

The more encouraging the situation or other cards in the spread, the easier it will be for you to orchestrate "happy endings" in matters. Like magic, your dexterity and resilience can enable you to get along more easily with even the most unusual and difficult people. This may be your chance to discover the truth about your standing in some matters, while preventing or undoing damage in others. Above all, you'll be able to recapture or reinforce your peace of mind.

The more challenging the situation or other cards in the spread the more likely you are to be your own worst enemy by NOT looking before you leap and *not* thinking before you speak. The harder other people try to please you, the more faults you can find with them and their efforts.

Key words:

Changeable /Incentive, Security

Card 30

The Four of Wands, Rods, Staves

Tip:

If this card appears in reverse (or upside-down) whatever your situation you may soon have cause to rethink your security.

Card thirty means: an opportunity to construct and complete matters in a manner that is as beneficial to others as yourself.

At your best, whatever your situation, by keeping your feet on the ground and viewing matters more realistically, you can attract sound opportunities for advancement.

Under more stressful conditions however, an overabundance of self-involvement, and self-interest may be blinding you to the fact in matters and keeping the happiness you seek just out of reach.

Card 31 the Five of Wands

Subject Card Five denotes conflict.

Unexpected events at work and at home could cause you to question yourself, your work, goals and/or the sincerity of people around you. Here the Wands desire to blaze their own trail becomes your trial by fire. Whatever the situation, whether it's being fueled by disappointment, provocation, or indecision – your biggest opponent is yourself. So sending your emotions to war against your logic may not be the best course of action.

The more encouraging the situation or other cards in the spread, the easier it will be for you to behave honorably, perhaps even volunteering to do more, when you'd planned to do less. No matter how upset you may be about something (or someone), you'll resist the temptation to overstep your bounds. Be glad you did, even if you could get away with misbehaving. Once you're free of whatever emotions you're wrestling with now, you'll be ready and able to accomplish anything! By taking the time to laugh at yourself and matters, instead of taking everything seriously, you'll find it easier than you expected to make up for whatever time (or money) you may have lost – which may not be as much as you anticipated.

The more challenging the situation or other cards in the spread, the more likely you or other people will make matters harder than they have to be. You may use you're dissatisfaction with one matter as an excuse to start an argument about something else. It may seem impossible to make up your mind. The harder it is for you to get along with yourself, the harder it will be for others to get along with you.

Key words:

Changeable/Conflict

Card 31

The Five of Wands, Rods, Staves

Tip:

If this card appears in reverse (or upside-down) it signifies ongoing conflict. It may seem as if the moment you rid yourself of one problem you're confronted by another. Enlisting additional self-control will help to see you through.

Card thirty-one means: Whatever your situation, the less time and energy you spend arguing with yourself, the sooner you can regain better control of yourself, matters – or both!

At your best, the better you feel about yourself, the greater your physical and mental energy will be. Thus, the less likely you are to incur any permanent setbacks, or lose anything you cannot easily live without.

Under more stressful conditions however, your insistence upon burning yourself out in no-win situations could be why you can neither relax nor get ahead.

Card 32 the Six of Wands

Subject Card Six challenges and rewards your willingness to keep matters running more efficiently and harmoniously.

Events at work and at home will provide unexpected opportunities for you to demonstrate your leadership, friendship, loyalty and co-operation. Taking proper advantage of these opportunities could boost your self-esteem and your status. Since the Six of Wands is an auspicious card that can suddenly bring you into contact with people who are in a position to assist you or advance your interests, it can be especially favorable for those with professional or political aspirations.

The more encouraging the situation or other cards in the spread, the easier you can achieve any number of victories with, or for other people at work and at home. Enlisting and extending assistance will help make everyone's agenda easier and more enjoyable. Should circumstances force you to co-operate with or contact someone you're uncomfortable with, or who is uncomfortable with you, you might discover you have more in common than you thought. You might be called on to negotiate a truce between opposing factions at work or at home. Socially, this is an ideal time to take advantage of any opportunities to join positive club or group endeavors. This is the right time to meet new people and solidify existing relationships. No matter where you are you may have a better time than you expected.

The more challenging the situation or other cards in the spread, whatever your situation you will continue to resist offers of assistance as well as advice and suggestions that could help improve matters for you. The tendency to become self-righteous can undermine even the most honorable goals.

Key words:

Changeable/ Commitment

Card 32

The Six of Wands, Rods, Staves

Tip:

If this card appears in reverse (or upside-down) your gains may be delayed or not as large as you expected.

Card thirty-two means: Teamwork. As long as you're comfortable with, and are confident about your endeavor, you're sure to attract or recruit the best people or partners .

At your best, you instinctively know how and when to attract an audience and hold their attention. You enjoy helping others and you welcome friendly competition.

Under more stressful conditions however, you can turn your charisma on and off like a faucet. The more certain you are of others' loyalty, favor or affection the more you may take them for granted.

Card 33 the Seven of Wands

Subject Card Seven corresponds to your personal and professional associations.

Thanks to the unique mix of opportunities and obstacles that karma and circumstance are about to toss into your path, you're going to need a little more persistence to reach your goals – no matter how simple or complex they may be. The good news is that your sense of humor and fair play can provide an unbeatable advantage by lending you whatever extra patience and energy you may need. The more often you replenish your energies through optimism and faith, the easier you can reject the pessimism that could spoil your mood as well as whatever matters you hope to promote. Events at work and home will provide unexpected opportunities to re-evaluate and make beneficial changes in your relationships.

The more encouraging the situation or other cards in the spread, the more your advice or assistance will be required and the more likely you may have to rearrange your agenda and reconsider your priorities. A soothing manner can make it virtually impossible for others to remain in a bad mood in your company, enabling you to achieve a mutual understanding more easily. At work and home, taking a direct yet non-threatening approach will inspire others to try and work harder or correct their mistakes, without feeling that you are pushing or judging them.

The more challenging the situation or other cards in the spread, although you may consider yourself the victim, you may be the perpetrator of your own unhappiness – perhaps by refusing to abandon familiar thought patterns and habits that are doing you more harm than good. Knowing when to throw away psychological and emotional crutches and doing it are two different matters.

Key words:

Changeable/ Relationships

Card 33

The Seven of Wands, Rods, Staves

Tip:

If this card appears in reverse (or upside-down) you may not be as adaptable as you imagine – or perhaps your adaptability is reaching its limit. Either way you may need to reconsider your position.

BASTONI BATONS 7 WANDS BASTOS

STÄBE STAVEN

Card thirty-three means: Adaptability. The more adaptable you are, the more you stand to gain in matters. The less adaptable you are, the longer you'll have to contend with upsetting circumstances.

At your best, you can bring matters out in the open in a manner that offends no one and benefits everyone.

Under more stressful conditions however, you can sometimes take your frustrations out on others without realizing it.

Card 34 the Eight of Wands

Subject Card Eight stands for renovation.

No matter how certain you are of where you're going and what you're doing whether by choice, or necessity you're about to take a step back from matters you're working on to adjust the accuracy of your focus. Unexpected events at work and home will instigate the need to move more quickly to complete, salvage or launch current matters in order to accommodate new matters. You may need to take an unplanned trip, or devise a new route or method of travel in your daily routine. Whatever the cause, you may suddenly feel as if matters are running away with you and over you, making it harder it to absorb everything that's happening.

The more encouraging the situation or other cards in the spread, the more you will accomplish in less time than you expected. Necessity is the mother of invention and you will be at your innovative best making sound decisions and completing your regular chores properly in less time than usual. Personally, professionally (or both) you may become an overnight success or sensation. One or more pieces of good news could leave you feeling better and more confident (or desirable!) than you have in some time.

The more challenging the situation or other cards in the spread means, perhaps, you've never mastered your temper. Perhaps you've never taken the time to realize which matters you should let go of sooner and which you should hold onto longer. Perhaps you're simply too quick to imagine the worst. Whatever the situation, the less certain you are of where you're going in life the sooner you realize it's you, not life that must change, the sooner you can transform your behavior and attitude from being part of the problem into becoming part of the solution.

key words:

Changeable/ Renovation

Card 34

The Eight of Wands, Rods, Staves

Tip:

If this card appears in re-verse (or upside-down) whatever your situation, whether or not you'd been expecting them to, matters may begin mov-ing more quickly, than you are prepared to deal with.

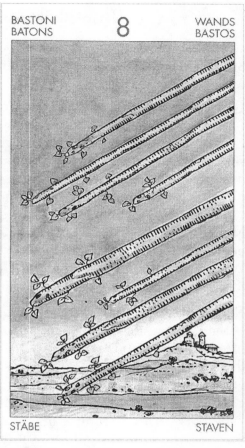

Card thirty-four means: at this time very few matters will fol-low prescribed guidelines and rules. Expect the unexpected in yourself, matters and other people now.

At your best, Your opportunistic nature, positive attitude and bold maneuvers can insure success.

Under more stressful conditions however, the harder you've tried to believe that happy endings create themselves, the more disappointed you may be.

Card 35 the Nine of Wands

Subject Card Nine represents understanding.

Unexpected events at work and home could tax your physical stamina. Whether you've encountered a number of close calls or taken a few hard falls in recent matters, it's time to reassess your values and change the habits that brought you to this impasse. With the Nine of Wands, you always gain something of value from your experiences once you learn to relax and go with the flow – even when the tide seems to be against you. The Nine of Wands is not a quitter – nor should you be. It simply bears out the old adage that everything happens for a reason. Whatever you learn now, can be the catalyst that inspires you to try again or seek a better direction.

The more encouraging the situation or other cards in the spread, the easier it will be for you to grasp the positive essence of whatever lessons you've learned, or are learning. Whatever the situation, your new outlook can enhance the practicality of your thinking, enabling your emotions and imagination to begin working for (rather than against) what you hope to achieve. Whether you are hoping to make a comeback or a debut, taking matters one step at time and not trying to look or plan too far ahead will aid you in replenishing your confidence and energy, as you begin to move forward.

The more challenging the situation or other cards in the spread, the harder it may be for you to make the changes that you know you need to make. You may be in danger of falling back into habits, attitudes and situations that could hamper your advancement. Depression can trigger a disconnection between your emotions and reality.

Key words:

Changeable/Unde rstanding

Card 35

The Nine of Wands

Tip:

If this card appears in re-verse (or upside-down) whatever your situation, you'd be especially wise to rethink matters before making any changes now. You probably have more options than you realize or are willing to consider.

Card thirty-five means: victory after a struggle.

At your best, each victory you score against pessimism and procrastination transforms one more stumbling block into a stepping stone that brings you closer to achieving your goals.

Under more stressful conditions however, the greater your sense of loss or confusion, the more distance you may put be-tween your feelings and the facts.

Card 36 the Ten of Wands

Subject Card Ten is a card for Achievement. It can also generate "instant karma" that can suddenly change the course of events for better or worse.

Situations at work and at home will provide you with sudden opportunities to make changes that can redirect the course of your life for the better – if you're not afraid to try. Whatever the situation; you're at a crossroads concerning your ability to absorb and work with any additional stress and tension. For whatever reason, the life-or-death intensity that you have attached to matters is transforming your powers of endurance into more of a hang-up than an advantage.

The more encouraging the situation or other cards in the spread, the more you will welcome, and work with, the chance to make changes that can improve the way you think, work or feel. The more positive your attitude, the stronger your ability to remain focused on the positive aspects in matters and make the impossible possible when you least expect it. From jobs to relationships, the better your reasons for letting go, or saying no, the sooner you can find something better – whether or not you're looking for change.

The more challenging the situation or other cards in the spread the easier you can devise excuses for remaining in the same old rut and breaking promises you've made to other people and yourself. The more cynical or apprehensive your attitude, the more often you will misconstrue the facts and meanings in matters. This can create more problems in your mind than really exist in the issues at hand. The more you doubt yourself the more important it is to defend and preserve whatever illusions you have created.

Keywords:

Changeable/ Achievement

Card 36

The Ten of Wands, Rods, Staves

Tip:

If this card appears in reverse (or upside-down) whatever your situation, perhaps you are the only one that is expecting too much from yourself.

Card thirty-six means: Endurance. Your personal drive and motivation may be somewhat lackadaisical now.

At your best, by remaining focused on what you really want to do, be or have, you can avoid feeling disheartened or blowing smaller issues out of proportion.

Under more stressful conditions however, feeling or believing that you're doomed to carry the weight of the world on your shoulders could start to become a bad habit.

CHAPTER 4

The Cups

The Cups - Emotions

Keyword: <u>Emotions</u>

Element: <u>Water</u>

Corresponding Astrological Signs: ♓ Pisces, ♋ Cancer, & ♏ Scorpio.

Corresponding Playing Card: Hearts.

Cups indicate the impact that your feelings will have upon matters.

Like the Water Signs, Cups promote the feelings that nourish our behavior and our dreams. Cups are the strongest of all the suits in the Minor Arcana because they represent our emotions. Our emotions dictate our ability to preserve, erode, reveal or redefine the truth about ourselves, and everything in our life. Cups also represent Sensitivity and Intuition. Each person's level of sensitivity enhances or diminishes their awareness of, and feelings for, everything and everyone. The more encouraging the situation or the other cards in the spread, the more logically you can deal with your feelings, share them and rely on their accuracy. Sometimes emotion can help us accomplish a matter when our physical strength or courage is depleted. The more challenging the situation or other cards in the spread the easier and more quickly your feelings could override your commonsense. Sometimes emotion can impel us to begin or pursue matters that we'd be wiser and better off to leave alone. If the majority of the spread consists of Cups, the matters at hand may prove to be more complex than they appear, or your manner of handling them may be more emotional than the matter itself. The more quickly you make up your mind, the harder it may be to follow the course of action you resolve to take.

Card 37 the King of Cups

Kings can trigger or enhance your personal initiative.

The King of Cups lends you the cunning of a Scorpio, the obscurity of a Pisces and the sense of duty of a Cancer to provide you with a truly unique approach to obtaining your objectives and frustrating your adversaries.

The more encouraging the situation or the other cards in the spread, whatever the situation, it will seem as if you can actually accomplish more by doing less. Many matters will seem to fall into place just as you'd hoped, and apparently of their own accord. Meetings or interviews with authority figures are likely to go quite smoothly as you can direct the flow along any path you choose. At work and at home people seem to anticipate your wishes by willingly complying with any special requests you may have. The happier you are, the happier everyone around you seems to be. You may contact or be contacted by people at a distance bearing good news related to your personal or professional affairs.

The more challenging the situation or the other cards in the spread the less willing people will be to comply with your agenda. The harder you try to regain control of matters, the more control seems to elude you. Meetings or interviews with authority figures are likely to prove counterproductive.

Romantically: Should your spread contain a hint of romance, you may begin to realize that you've been alone too long, or that you care more deeply for someone than you were aware of.

The more reassuring the situation or other cards in the spread, the more likely the attraction will be mutual.

The less reassuring the situation or other cards in the spread, the more complex and possibly less rewarding your relationship will be.

Key words:

Emotional / Initiative

Card 37

The King of Cups, Goblets, Chalices

Tip:

If this card appears in reverse (or upside-down) it signifies initiative that may be lacking in sincerity.

RE DI COPPE
ROI DE COUPES
KING OF CHALICES
REY DE COPAS

KÖNIG DER KELCHE   BEKERS KONING

Card thirty-seven means: When necessary, your chameleon-like ability to camouflage yourself and matters can enable you to zoom to the top in every instance – no matter how far down you may have started or allowed yourself to be pushed.

At your best, your positive character, shrewd judgment and natural caring enable you to tackle your responsibilities with an open mind and a sense of fun – almost as if you were planning a picnic.

Under more stressful conditions however, it can be as easy for you to lie to yourself as to other people.

Card 38 the Queen of Cups

Queens can enhance your charisma and people-skills.

Your ability to set and follow a separate, (not necessarily secret) agenda can help you retain your objectivity and prevent problems from overwhelming you. Although you often draw new strength from opposition, your ability to camouflage yourself and blend in with people and situations, whenever you feel uncertain, can sometimes be your guardian angel.

The more encouraging the situation or the other cards in the spread, the more inspirational your example will prove to be. At work and at home you can please and charm everyone with a smile or a glance. You emit a positive yet soothing effect that makes everyone feel more alive and confident. Without even trying, you can breathe new life and hope into dead issues, solve perplexing problems and settle quarrels to everyone's satisfaction. People who can further your interests seem to appear out of nowhere – ready to oblige.

The more challenging the situation or other cards in the spread, the more you could use your influence and impact to deliberately spoil or delay matters for other people. The harder you try to mask your irritability, or unhappiness, the more obvious and contagious it becomes.

Romantically: Should your spread contain a hint of romance, you could soon meet the love of your life, or begin an infatuation that controls your life.

The more reassuring the situation or other cards in the spread, romance may change your entire approach to life with positive results.

The less reassuring the situation or the other cards in the spread the more disruptive your relationship may be.

Key words:

Emotional Charisma

Card 38

The Queen of Cups, Goblets, Chalices

Tip:

If this card appears in reverse (or upside-down) it can signal charisma combined with an abundance of self-interest.

REGINA DI COPPE
REINE DE COUPES

QUEEN OF CHALICES
REINA DE COPAS

KÖNIGIN DER KELCHE   BEKERS KONINGIN

Card thirty-eight means: You are very analytical (sometimes even calculating) and you don't like losing. At work and home, you can choose to be the catalyst for unity or disharmony.

At your best, your no-nonsense behavior is coupled with a caring attitude. You never rely on one matter or person to be your answer to everything. You enjoy people who are not afraid to be themselves.

Under more stressful conditions however, sometimes your diversity can cause others to feel you're not taking your commitments seriously. You may require some time alone to refresh both your perspective and inner self.

Card 39 the Knight of Cups

Knights indicate unexpected developments in matters or your behavior.

Each Knight has the potential to trigger a different type of behavior. The Knight Of Cups can lend you just the right amount of diplomacy or psychological subtlety to outwit an opponent or win your hearts desire. The greater your determination to succeed in life the more likely you will win your objective through a combination of hard work and incredibly smooth moves.

The more encouraging the situation or the other cards in the spread, the greater your willingness to let bygones be bygones and tackle matters that you normally dislike with a cheery attitude. Your humorous approach to matters that interrupt your agenda enables you to maintain your schedule. A number of pleasant social invitations or professional proposals could come your way – like magic. You're particularly intuitive now and your dreams may be more precognitive.

The more challenging the situation or other cards in the spread the more challenging it may be to talk your way out of any matters you've mishandled. The more charming, or agreeable you try to be, the less impressed and more annoyed other people seem to be. At work and at home matters that were going well may begin to disintegrate before your eyes with no explanation. Travel or social plans could change or fall through at the last minute.

Romantically: Should your spread contain a hint of romance,

The more reassuring the other cards in spread, the more likely it is that you could fall in love more quickly than you expected or intended.

The less reassuring the situation or the other cards in the spread the more likely it is that you, or the object of your affection are not being completely honest with one another.

Key words:

Emotional Adventure

Card 39

The Knight of Cups, Goblets, Chalices

Tip:

If this card appears in reverse (or upside-down) whatever the situation, beware the temptation to lull yourself into a false sense of security.

CAVALLO DI COPPE · KNIGHT OF CHALICES
CHEVALIER DE COUPES · CABALLO DE COPAS

RITTER DER KELCHE · BEKERS RIDDER

Card thirty-nine means: The greater your determination to win, the easier you can wend your way through other peoples hypocrisy and double standards, to obtain your goals.

At your best, your ability to understand others so well, stems from your willingness to be honest with yourself, and learn from your mistakes. You prefer coercing your opponents to challenging them.

Under more stressful conditions however, there may be very little sincerity behind your promises or any depth of affection that you claim to possess.

Card 40 the Page of Cups

Pages signal small matters with the potential to grow larger.

The Page of Cups signals an emotional turning point – for better or worse. At work and at home you'll become more aware of how much and why you like or dislike certain people and matters.

The more encouraging the situation or the other cards in the spread, the easier it will be for you to address and express your feelings rather than deny them. You'll feel more self-confident about handling matters you've been avoiding. You may be more receptive to the idea of becoming pregnant or considering adoption, seeking better employment, or beginning a new hobby, whether as a means of broadening your social horizons or some much needed personal relaxation.

The more challenging the situation or other cards in the spread the harder it may be to resist delivering or responding to ultimatums that could do more harm than good. Smaller annoyances or disagreements could rapidly escalate into fully fledged confrontations. Family turmoil could bring the responsibility of a "little someone" that you didn't expect, to your door.

Romantically: Should your spread contain a hint of romance, you'll discover that your feelings for someone are changing.

The more reassuring the other cards in spread, the more likely you could feel that a friendship is capable of becoming more. You may feel as if you're starting to fall in love all over again with your current mate or partner. You may become more interested in meeting new people socially.

The less reassuring the situation or other cards in the spread the more you may feel as if continuing your present relationship would be a mistake.

Key words:

Emotional Surprises

Card 40

The Page of Cups, Goblets, Chalices

Tip:

If this card appears in reverse (or upside-down) whatever the situation, problems in your emotional life could begin to affect in your professional life or professional problems could begin to unbalance matters in your personal life.

Card forty means: the dawn of a new era – an inevitable turning point, where one or more matters that have gone on so long in one direction will now begin to change course.

At your best, you can be forthright without being too forward. You can be a good listener and your ability to discern truth from falsehood can enable you to stay one step ahead in matters. You enjoy pitting your wits and energies against life's challenges.

Under more stressful conditions however, a tendency to exaggerate, fostered by the desire to appear more important or knowledgeable than you are, only creates fresh problems.

Card 41 the Ace of Cups

Aces represent crisis or reward.

The more encouraging the situation or the other cards in the spread, the more grateful, relieved or thankful you'll feel about a new turn of events at work or at home. You may feel as if a cloud or burden that you've been laboring under has been lifted. You'll feel more charitable and understanding towards other people. You may even be more creative or outgoing than ever before. Your premonitions and dreams could be uncommonly strong – and accurate. Keeping an open heart and mind can help prevent your emotions from getting the better of your commonsense. Retaining some degree of personal freedom to express as well as experience your emotions is essential to achieving a harmonious blend and balance between your emotions and behavior.

The more challenging the situation or other cards in the spread the greater the risk of making matters worse or borrowing additional trouble by trying to force things to go your way. You may be too emotional to see matters clearly.

Romantically: Should your spread contain a hint of romance, it may be virtually impossible to keep your feelings to yourself.

The more reassuring the other cards in the spread, the more likely you may receive or deliver a proposal of marriage or passionate declaration of love. You could renew your marriage vows, surprise or be surprised by an overwhelmingly romantic gift or gesture. You may soon become a willing victim of love at first sight.

The less reassuring the situation or the other cards in the spread the more likely you and/or your loved one are to have a bitter and hurtful quarrel. You may feel as if you're being emotionally overwhelmed.

Key word:

Crisis/Reward

Card 41

The Ace of Cups,
Goblets.

Tip:

If this card appears in reverse (or upside-down) it will be more challenging to come to grips with your emotions as well as any emotional negativity that you encounter.

Card forty-one means: whatever the situation, by working more constructively with your emotions now, you can make this time period more productive and rewarding.

At your best, you don't have to pin down exactly where your feelings come from every moment. Your emotions help you enhance – not escape the reality of life. Your contagious and inspirational zest for life may encourage you to accomplish feats that leave others in awe.

Under more stressful conditions however, the stronger your cynicism or self-pity the more jealous, possessive or self-indulgent you can become.

Card 42 the Two of Cups

Subject Card Two signifies interaction.

Events that take place at work, at home, or both, will strengthen your affection and loyalty, or suspicion and irritation with people.

The more encouraging the situation or the other cards in the spread, the easier it will be for you and other people to understand and relate to one another harmoniously. At work, home or both you can combine your organizational abilities and people skills more effectively than ever. Even the most reticent people will feel more confident, positive and alive, in your company. You'll feel less threatened by other people's independence, less hesitant to exercise your own initiative. You'll also be more receptive to any good suggestions or advice. The more supportive you are of other peoples endeavors, the more willingly they'll endorse your projects. The good impressions you make reflect how good you feel.

The more challenging the situation or other cards in the spread the more you may feel as if everyone is against you or trying to patronize you. Your feelings of irritation or uncertainty could contaminate even the jolliest atmosphere at work and at home – causing everyone to feel uneasy.

Romantically: The more reassuring the other cards in spread, the greater your social opportunities for romantic possibilities. Sharing your hobbies and interests with your mate or partner can make you a perfect "party of two."

The less reassuring the situation or other cards in the spread the more likely it is that you and the object of your affection will disagree about a particular matter or course of action.

Key words:

Emotional/ Interaction

Card 42

The Two of Cups, Goblets,Chalices.

Tip:

If this card appears in reverse (or upside-down) whatever the situation, matters or people that you thought you couldn't get along without, may suddenly annoy you to no end.

Card forty-two means: whatever the situation, whatever you're feeling, can enable you to be a more formidable opponent or powerful ally than either you or other people may expect.

At your best, you're as attracted to positive people and endeavors or organizations as they are to you. Your ability to simultaneously strike the right chord with some people while hitting the wrong note with others can lend a note of sparkling controversy to your popularity.

Under more stressful conditions however, you'd be wise to avoid people and entertainments that bring out your worst – instead of your best traits.

Card 43 the Three of Cups

Subject Card Three is for thinking and networking.

Events at work and home will provide ample opportunities for you and other people to express and discuss your feelings. You are fueled by the determination to find a better way or a better answer as well as a need to know, see and do as much as possible. Whatever the situation, your desire to share and process ideas and information can make it easier to develop new approaches and techniques concerning matters from finance to romance and everything in between!

The more encouraging the situation or the other cards in the spread, the easier it will be to resolve any potential or genuine misunderstandings. You'll feel particularly communicative now, ready to listen with an open mind and respond with sincerity, clarity and diplomacy. People "in the know" are inclined to share information and take the time to listen and talk with you. You may reach a decision or receive news that deserves a night on the town or a weekend getaway. You may host or attend a gathering or even become the recipient of an award, prize or trip.

The more challenging the situation or other cards in the spread the more carefully you should check your timing and your facts before believing or disbelieving anything you hear and especially what you feel.

Romantically: The more reassuring the situation or other cards in spread, the more likely you could meet someone special, perhaps through a friend whether by accident or prearrangement.

The less reassuring the situation or the other cards in the spread, the more likely you and the object of your affection may try to incite each other's jealousy – perhaps without realizing it.

Key words:

Emotional/ Thinking,Networking

Card 43

The Three of Cups, Goblets,Chalices.

Tip:

If this card appears in reverse (or upside-down) whatever the situation, you or someone close to you may be guilty of embellishing the truth or failing to keep a secret.

Card forty-three means: Sharing. At home and work all sorts of gossip as well as a few nuggets of pertinent information will soon be traveling your way.

At your best, by listening to or sympathizing with everyone, but siding with no one, you can remain in every ones good graces without becoming any ones fool. Others can rely on you to keep your word and their secrets.

Under more stressful conditions however, whatever the situation, your imagination may lead you to believe that other people are always fighting over you – or with you, and that someone else is the only cause or answer to your dilemmas.

Card 44 Four of Cups

Subject Card Four stands for incentive and security.

Events at work and at home will trigger feelings of anxiety or self-satisfaction relating to people and matters you feel are necessary for your well being. Whatever the situation, you are being stimulated by a unique blend of material and emotional elements. So, whether or not you're more intuitive now, you're definitely more aware of certain possibilities and pitfalls that others either can't or won't see. This can enable you to plan ahead for any problems that might arise.

The more encouraging the situation or the other cards in the spread, the happier you'll feel about your job, material security and your role in your relationships. A number of pleasant possibilities for increasing your material security and emotional satisfaction are within your grasp. The greater your desire to move forward in life, the easier you can devise a more effective course of action that will enhance your resourcefulness, spirituality and creativity.

The more challenging the situation or other cards in the spread the more uncertain you may feel about the present and the future. You may question the wisdom of your recent choices or behavior. This is not a good time to concoct believable excuses. Avoid the temptation to get carried away by feelings of "would-have, should-have, and could-have". They will make it more challenging to untangle your feelings.

Romantically: The more reassuring the situation or other cards in spread, the easier you can stop living in the past or avoid repeating your past mistakes.

The less reassuring the situation or the other cards in the spread, the harder it may be to put your past disappointments behind you, and believe that the best is yet to come – although it is.

Key words:

Emotional/Incentive, Security

Card 44

The Four of Cups, Goblets, Chalices.

Tip:

If this card appears in reverse (or upside-down) you may be in denial or taking too much for granted – whether by refusing to believe matters could change or refusing to accept they have changed.

Card forty-four means: taking a "leap of faith" whether in yourself, others, matters – or all three.

At your best, you won't allow your own or others' insecurities to influence your decisions. Being in touch with your "higher self" lends you the courage to follow what "feels right" to you whether or not everyone else approves or understands.

Under more stressful conditions however, you may feel it's impossible for you to relax, or seek (and follow) even the most reliable advice or medical assistance until either your work is done or your dilemma resolved.

Card 45 the Five of Cups

Subject Card Five denotes conflict.

Events at work and at home could cause you to question yourself, your work, goals and/or the sincerity of people around
you. Encouraging yourself to take more satisfaction in the
present, and be happy with who you are will bolster your
self-confidence about the future.

The more encouraging the situation or the other cards in the
spread, the easier it will be for you to avoid melancholy by giving yourself something positive to look forward to. This is especially important if you're grappling with a recent setback or
emotional disappointment. The more you give yourself to look
forward to, the easier you can keep the past in perspective and
confront the present. The more diversified your interests, the
easier you can keep moving forward.

The more challenging the situation or other cards in the spread
developing a "what's-the-use" attitude or behavior will only increase your worry. The more you believe you can do for other
people the more you'll realize they must do it for themselves. The
more you expect people to do for you the more you'll have to do
for yourself. The sooner you accept any disturbing premonitions
or dreams that you might have, as an "early warning system," the
sooner you can conquer any anxiety they may cause you. Talking
with a friend or perhaps a professional counselor could help.

Romantically: The more reassuring the situation or other
cards in the spread, the easier it may be to resolve an emotional
misunderstanding or achieve a mutual parting.

The less reassuring the other cards in the spread, the more important it is that you don't backslide into self-defeating habits or
relationships. Talking with a friend or perhaps a professional
counselor could help.

Key words:

Emotional/Conflict

Card 45

The Five of Cups, Goblets, Chalices.

Tip:

If this card appears in reverse (or upside-down) you should beware of becoming too involved (or re-involved) with people or matters or habits that will only disappoint you.

Card forty-five means: Melancholy. Whatever the situation, your awareness of the past does not have to keep you chained to it.

At your best, you're reflective, resourceful and very conscientious about "reaping what you sow." Whenever you feel pressured you avoid taking your frustration out on other people, by withdrawing temporarily – whether to meditate, rethink your strategy or revitalize your energy.

Under more stressful conditions however, expecting the worst only sets you up for your next disappointment and makes it easier to dig yourself deeper into matters and moods you've been trying to get out of.

Card 46 the Six of Cups

Subject Card Six challenges and rewards your willingness to keep matters running efficiently and harmoniously.

Some events at work and at home may provide overdue vindication, or perhaps an opportunity to receive or express heartfelt appreciation. Other events may trigger feelings of nostalgia. Unbidden thoughts and memories from your past will play small but significant roles in the manner you handle your present concerns and chart your future. Good deeds you've done in the past, that seemed to go unnoticed, could bear fruit now. Whatever the situation, you may encounter one or more inexplicable episode of deja'vu, pre-cognitive dreams or eerily accurate hunches.

The more encouraging the situation or other cards in the spread, the more likely you are to hear something from, or about, someone from your past. You may meet someone or travel to someplace that feels "familiar" to you although you've never seen them before now. Avenues and opportunities that were closed are beginning to open.

The more challenging the situation or the other cards in the spread the more likely a past indiscretion, oversight or minor medical issue could resurface, to your disadvantage.

Romantically: The more reassuring the situation or other cards in spread, the more likely your relationship could be changing for the better. You may resume a former relationship. You may receive an opportunity to date someone you've been interested in for a while; or you may give someone a chance to date you.

The less reassuring the other cards in spread, the more likely you are to wonder if what you have to show for your social life or in your relationship is really worth everything you've put yourself through to maintain it.

Key words:

Emotional/ Commitment

Card 46

The Six of Cups, Goblets,Chalices.

Tip:

If this card appears in reverse (or upside-down) you may soon be contacted by or have cause to contact someone you'd been hoping avoid.

Card forty-six means: Nostalgia.Taking a closer look at how far you've come and counting your blessings.

At your best, knowing that you are doing the best you can – in the best way possible for all concerned refresh your faith and strengthen your ability to keep working towards a brighter tomorrow.

Under more stressful conditions however, the greater your preoccupation with the more negative elements of your past and present the less you need to wonder why your future appears so bleak. Talking with a friend, religious advisor or professional counselor could help.

Card 47 the Seven of Cups

Subject Card Seven corresponds to your personal and professional associations.

Events at work and at home will prompt you to re-evaluate one or more of your relationships – for better or worse. One matter going askew could put your entire agenda "up in the air" – for better or worse.

The more encouraging the situation or other cards in the spread, the easier it will be to rearrange matters in order of their importance. You may be pleasantly surprised to discover that you have more free time than you expected.

The more challenging the situation or other cards in the spread the more likely it is that you'll have to make apologies, or excuses, or even substitute for someone at work, at home, or both. Your talent for making matters appear to be as you wish they were can sometimes convince everyone that you're telling the truth – when nothing could be farther from the truth. The longer you ignore or deny issues you don't want to confront, the harder it will be to stay focused on the matters you enjoy.

Romantically: The more reassuring the situation or other cards in spread, the more likely it is that you'll discover you have more social and romantic options than you had imagined. Your social adaptability and versatility make you a welcome addition to any gathering.

The less reassuring the other cards in spread, the more likely it is that you could make two dates for the same day without realizing it! Something you've heard or seen, or said and done, may raise questions or doubts that need to be addressed now.

Key words:

Emotional/ Relationships

Card 47

The Seven of Cups, Goblets, Chalices.

Tip:

If this card appears in reverse (or upside-down) circumstances may soon cause you to feel as if you're running a day late and a dollar short, often making it in just under the wire in matters.

COPPE COUPES · 7 · CHALICES COPAS

KELCHE   BEKERS

Card forty-seven means: Uncertainty. You're about to discover that you've over, or under estimated something – or someone for better or worse.

At your best, the more practical and realistic you are, the easier and more often you can transform losing matters into winning propositions – much to the consternation of your adversaries and the delight of your supporters.

Under more stressful conditions however, your insistence on putting "too many irons" in the fire, you cost yourself more than if you'd taken the time to handle matters more realistically.

Card 48 the Eight of Cups

Subject Card Eight stands for renovation.

This is a card that can symbolize emotional transformation, or a spiritual reawakening – and sometimes both. This is the individualist. Events at work and at home will promote awareness that you have not been making the most of yourself.

The more encouraging the situation or other cards in the spread, the easier it will be for you to resolve conflicting emotions that have been undermining your individuality and progress. You're more ready and willing than ever before to make your own decisions and find your own way in matters. It may be easier than you expected to salvage, or take charge of, or walk away from matters, habits (or people) that aren't good for you.

The more challenging the situation or other cards in the spread the more work you have ahead of you to discover who you are and what you want. Once you can distinguish the significant from the insignificant, you can separate fact from fantasy more easily and become more appreciative of your individuality and purpose in life. Prayer, meditation or even strenuous physical exercise could assist you in beginning your positive transformation more easily.

Romantically: The more reassuring the situation or other cards in the spread, the easier it will be to leave the past in the past and make a fresh start whether by yourself or as a couple, or even with someone new.

The less reassuring the other cards in spread, the more likely it is that you've been wandering in emotional circles for some time. Speaking with a close friend, religious advisor or professional counselor could prevent you from repeating your past mistakes.

Key words:

Emotional/ Renovation

The Eight of Cups, Goblets, Chalices.

Tip:

If this card appears in reverse (or upside-down) working with the truth in matters may prove more challenging than you expected.

Card forty-eight means: Re-evaluation. Whatever your situation, administering a personal reality check can help refresh and maintain your inner balance and clarity of purpose.

At your best, you are your own person and happy to be so. Other people find your company as soothing as it is inspirational.

Under more stressful conditions however, you can give yourself an extraordinarily difficult time in life. Any spiritual, social, or emotional isolation you may be laboring under is largely self-imposed.

Card 49 the Nine of Cups

Subject Card Nine represents understanding.

This is the wish card. Since the Nine of Cups tends to set Karmic wheels in motion, you'd be especially wise to be careful what you wish for now. Events at work and/or at home will give you the feeling that it could be easier than you expected to get into or out of something. Your hopes may be higher than they've been for a while. Yet, no matter how strongly you desire something (or someone) now, facing the truth and/or handling the consequences should your wish come true may prove more challenging than you expect, or are prepared to handle.

The more encouraging the situation or the other cards in the spread, the easier it will be to get your own way with less effort or resistance than you expected. You could obtain a better deal, better job, or bigger promotion.

The more challenging the situation or other cards in the spread the more challenging it may be to uphold your ethics in the light of temptation. Something may turn out to be a great deal less than you expected. Self-indulgence can be your worst enemy whether you're overestimating or underestimating other people, matters or yourself!

Romantically: The more reassuring the situation or other cards in the spread, the easier it may be to obtain a date with, or impress, someone that interests you.

The less reassuring the other cards in the spread, the harder it may be to resist the temptation to stray or take unethical advantage of an emotional situation. It may be proving harder than you expected to free yourself from a relationship that no longer pleases you.

Key words:

Emotional/Understanding

The Nine of Cups, Goblets,Chalices.

Tip:

If this card appears in reverse (or upside-down) your wish may be delayed or prove not to be all that you expect.

Card forty-nine means: Desire. Be careful what you wish for.

At your best, your attitude is positive and generally optimistic. Commonsense is your guide, making your wishes easier to attain and retain because they are more practical and realistic than idealistic.

Under more stressful conditions however, beware of allowing your ego to overwhelm your common sense.

Card 50 the Ten of Cups

Subject Card Ten is a card for Achievement. It can also generate "instant karma" that can suddenly change the course of events for better or worse.

Events at work and/or at home will heighten your feelings about, memories of, or longing for, togetherness. The less restricted you feel by anyone person or matter the more good you can accomplish for all.

The more encouraging the situation or the other cards in the spread, the easier it will be for you and other people to compromise – possibly for the sake of a larger issue. You may take the first step towards healing an emotional breach. This can bring good news and good times together. You can make even the most tedious task more enjoyable. It may be almost impossible to determine where your friends begin and family ends.

The more challenging the situation or the other cards in the spread the more complex or hopeless matters may seem to be. This can signal emotional disharmony or loss. People who should be closest to you may seem to be deliberately pitting themselves against you and your mutual endeavors. Speaking with a close friend, religious advisor or professional counselor could help you adjust your perspective, or prevent you from making matters worse.

Romantically: The more reassuring the situation or other cards in the spread, the more you stand to gain from positive social interaction. You could meet your future partner or mate. You may become engaged or get married. This can signal a happy pregnancy or birth.

The less reassuring the other cards in the spread, the less likely you and your mate or partner will be able to avoid a serious disagreement or separation. There may be news of an unexpected pregnancy.

Key words:

Emotional/ Achievement

The Ten of Cups, Goblets, Chalices.

Tip:

If this card appears in reverse (or upside-down) whatever your situation, you may be in for a rude awakening.

Card fifty means: life *is* what *you* make it.

At your best, you can resolve your differences of opinion constructively, in a manner that helps you and those you care for to continue to get ahead – even when you're moving in opposite directions. Everything you do expresses the joy you feel for life.

Under more stressful conditions however, your "need to be needed" or an inability to resist some form of temptation may prove to be your Achilles heel and possibly lead to your undoing.

CHAPTER 5

The Swords

The Swords: Challenge

Keyword: <u>Challenge</u>

Element: <u>Air</u>

Corresponding Astrological Signs:

♒ Aquarius, ♊ Gemini, & ♎ Libra.

Corresponding Playing Card: Spades

Swords indicate the effect that communications coming to you or from you will have on situations. Swords can sometimes accelerate or delay your plans. Swords make you stop and think – they engage your intellect.

Like the Air Signs, Swords exemplify our communication skills as well as our ideas, and self-control is the key that can transform any challenges or delays that you initiate or encounter into an opportunity to succeed. If you are reading the Universal or Rider-Waite Tarot Deck more often than not, when the Swords are upright you can think more clearly and you mindset may be more positive, enabling your communications to flow more smoothly – if not happily. However, when the Swords are pointing sideways there is a greater possibility of mis-communication—usually due to mixed signals, and when the Swords are pointing downwards they signal additional complications that can make it more challenging to attain or maintain a positive and focused mindset.

No matter what Tarot deck you choose, just remember that Swords imply tension that can impel you to behave too offensively or too defensively. Whatever the situation, you consider it to be a matter of principle.

The more encouraging the situation or other cards in the spread, you'll meet matters head-on displaying courage and determination, or humor and wisdom that may even surprise you! Your sense of justice, principle and integrity can bring order into chaos.

The more challenging the situation or other cards in the spread the more you will need to apply and rely on self-control to turn the tide of events in your favour – whether you're in danger of becoming too self-righteous or simply inclined to take too many risks. If the majority of the spread consists of Swords, your greatest challenge will be to remain focussed upon your ultimate goal. Swords can imply as much – if not more, distraction as inspiration.

Card 51 the King of Swords

Kings can trigger or enhance your personal initiative.

Whatever the situation the King of Swords can enable you to deal more comfortably with the facts in any situation. Even people with whom you seldom agree are likely to be more receptive to your advice, suggestions and opinions at this time.

The more encouraging the situation or other cards in the spread, the better prepared you will be to tackle each task and/or dilemma you encounter. At work and at home, you exude capability and readiness, moving from one matter to the next like a general executing a well-planned campaign. You're more likely to schedule and less likely to cancel any medical or dental appointments on your agenda. Although cordial, your manner is as determined as your behavior. Your direct manner can serve you well in meetings or interviews with authority figures.

The more challenging the situation or other cards in the spread the more likely you are to blame other people for your lack of focus and preparation. Meetings or interviews with authority figures are likely to prove counterproductive. You'll take too many matters personally or the wrong way. Your refusal to discuss matters will only compound any misunderstandings that arise.

Romantically: Should your spread contain a hint of romance, your determination to win the object of your affection could be handicapped by your reluctance to make the first move.

The more reassuring the situation or other cards in the spread, the more likely the attraction will be mutual, but not necessarily long-lived.

The less reassuring the situation or other cards in the spread the more challenging and intense your relationship will be because of the "mixed signals" you both employ.

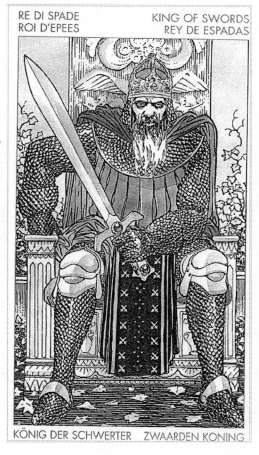

Key words:

Challenging Initiative

Card 51

The King of Swords, or Daggers.

Tip:

If this card appears in reverse (or upside-down) whatever your situation, you may soon discover that you placed your trust in the wrong person or people.

Card fifty-one means: since you are likely to be more outspoken now, it may be easier than usual for you to relate to other people who are the same way.

At your best, you can prove to be uncommonly resourceful and self-assertive should your path become blocked by unnecessary protocol or narrow-minded thinking and attitudes.

Under more stressful conditions however, the more anxious you are to gain the approval or support of other people, the more likely you are to mishandle matters and create the opposite effect.

Card 52 the Queen of Swords

Queens can enhance your charisma and people-skills.

Whatever your situation, you are as acquisitive as you are in-
quisitive – seeking to expand your knowledge and horizons
– yet extremely cautious about accepting any opportunity
without examining it more closely.

The more encouraging the situation or other cards in the spread,
the more awe-inspiring as well as positive your example will be.
At work and at home, you're the epitome of "If I can do it – anyone can" setting an example that's as inspirational as it is effective.
Whatever cause or idea you choose to promote or defend is certain to showcase your capabilities. Your awareness and intuitive
abilities have a keener edge that can help you avert disaster or ca-
lamity at the last possible moment.

The more challenging the situation or other cards in the spread
the more challenging the matters at hand will be. You must beware of putting more wheels in motion than you can control easily. You may have to "pay the piper" now for some type of rash
past behavior. At work, home or both you may soon discover that
someone has been playing a dual role of friend and foe in one of
your personal or professional relationships.

Romantically: Should your spread contain a hint of romance,
your determination to win the object of your affection could
cause you to misrepresent yourself.

The more reassuring the situation or other cards in the spread,
the more likely your attraction may be based upon mutual past
emotional disappointments.

The less reassuring the situation or other cards in the spread
the more you may enjoy the challenge of gaining others' affection more than the realities of the relationship.

Key words:

Challenging Charisma

Card 52

The Queen of Swords, or Daggers

Tip:

If this card appears in reverse (or upside-down) you may soon have to account for a matter you mishandled.

REGINA DI SPADE   QUEEN OF SWORDS
REINE D'EPEES   REINA DE ESPADAS

KÖNIGIN DER SCHWERTER   ZWAARDEN KONINGIN

Card fifty-two means: you're an efficient organizer and planner who can become irritable when your timetable is disrupted. Taking good care of your physical health should be first not last on your list.

At your best, you are a shrewd and accurate judge of your emotional and material concerns --always ready and able to negotiate or bargain your way to the top in any endeavor.

Under more stressful conditions however, time after time you can push other people and matters too far. One day you're a tyrant – the next you're a martyr.

Card 53 the Knight of Swords

Knights indicate unexpected developments in matters or your behavior.

Each Knight has the potential to trigger a different type of behavior. The Knight of Swords can enhance your determination and enable you to devise a multitude of winning strategies that are as unique as they are resourceful. Yet, no matter how flawless your strategy, you could still lose – unless your goal is more purposeful than pointless. The sooner you learn what is worth fighting for, the sooner you'll put your emotions to work for you rather than against you.

The more encouraging the situation or other cards in the spread, At work and at home, it may appear as if you're everywhere at once whenever you're needed. Your "can-do" energy will enable you to accomplish even more matters than you needed to. You'll appear to be as invincible as you feel – taking the helm in matter after matter whether to save the day or start the ball rolling!

The more challenging the situation or other cards in the spread the harder it will be to summon the energy and focus that you need to keep pace with matters at home and at work. The closer you come to an agreement, the harder it is to finalize matters. Health, dental, or legal emergencies could come out of nowhere. Disagreements could become too intense. Court dates may be delayed or changed without warning – or notice. Try to be more careful when traveling too; a ticket or a fender-bender could come out of nowhere.

Romantically: Should your spread contain a hint of romance,

The more reassuring the situation or other cards in the spread, the stronger, but not necessarily in synch your attraction for one another will be. You may surprise yourself by suddenly becoming engaged, moving in together or getting married.

The less reassuring the situation or other cards in the spread the more you will feel as if you're beating your head against a brick wall, whether you're trying to begin or end a relationship.

Key words:

Challenging Adventure

Card 53

The Knight of Swords, or Daggers

Tip:

If this card appears in reverse (or upside-down) whatever the situation you may soon have to admit you've been wasting more time, energy, emotion or money than you should have.

CAVALLO DI SPADE   KNIGHT OF SWORDS
CHEVALIER D'EPEES   CABALLO DE ESPADAS

RITTER DER SCHWERTER   ZWAARDEN RIDDER

Card fifty-three means: you'd be wise to choose your battles carefully.

At your best, your skillful manner and resourceful nature can make you appear to be both fearless and inexhaustible. A team player, your positive belief system is as contagious as it is inspirational – making you a powerful asset as well as a formidable adversary.

Under more stressful conditions however, even when you're in the best mood – one wrong word could spoil your day. You can become more frenzied than flexible.

Card 54 the Page of Swords

Pages signal small matters with the potential to grow larger.

When traveling you're sure to arrive either sooner or later than you expected. Beware of small accidents – especially on your own two feet.

The more encouraging the situation or other cards in the spread, the easier you can resolve smaller frustrations and disagreements without blowing matters out of proportion. At work and at home matters as well as your energy level will be a little more erratic and unpredictable. You'll get further ahead in the long run and come closer to maintaining your present agenda by setting small goals that are easier to accomplish.

The more challenging the situation or other cards in the spread the more likely you are to make a mountain out of a molehill. A small medical or dental problem could rapidly escalate into a major dilemma. So could a small financial oversight, legal matter or misunderstanding.

Romantically: Should your spread contain a hint of romance, the possibility of meeting someone new, or becoming closer to or further estranged from your current mate or partner is likely to stem from how each of you say whatever you say to one another in the near future.

The more reassuring the other cards in the spread, the more likely you are to experience a "meeting of the minds" or an "aha" moment of understanding and clarification. Witty – even quirky, or profound comments could be the catalyst that brings you closer together with other people.

The less reassuring the situation, or the other cards in the spread, the more likely you are to notice a slightly less appealing side of each other's character or personality that could serve as an early warning or the final straw.

Key words:

Challenging Surprises

Card 54

The Page of Swords, or Daggers

Tip:

If this card appears in reverse (or upside-down) whatever the situation, at work, home or both you may soon have to deal with a disagreement, that could take you by surprise.

FANTE DI SPADE
VALET D'EPEES
KNAVE OF SWORDS
SOTA DE ESPADAS

BUBE DER SCHWERTER   ZWAARDEN SCHILDKNAAP

Card fifty-four means: No matter how good any news that you receive may be, don't assume that your success is "in the bag". No matter how problematical any news that you receive may be, don't assume that all is lost.

At your best, you know how to make the "element of surprise" work for you! You temper your determination with diplomacy to get further ahead at a pace that's just right for you and everything you hope to accomplish.

Under more stressful conditions however, your child-like charm, contagious enthusiasm, or overall appeal, can mask a very conniving, cunning and callous nature.

Card 55 the Ace of Swords

Aces represent crisis or reward.

The more encouraging the situation or other cards in the spread, the more likely you are to emerge as the victor in matters at work or at home. Whatever the reason, you're ready to be more self-assertive. Whether or not everyone likes you, they'll have to respect your fortitude and they're sure to understand where you're coming from. This could bring news of a promotion at work, some type of legal or medical victory, or success in achieving a professional or publishing contract.

The more challenging the situation or other cards in the spread the more likely you are to encounter an unexpected legal, medical or dental emergency – or job crisis whether for you or someone close to you.

Romantically: It's not unusual for the Ace of Swords to represent a relationship or attraction where one or both parties appear to be waiting for the other to make a choice, a decision or the first move.

Should your spread contain a hint of romance, whether or not you are romantically involved, this is a time when you can more easily identify and come to terms with any "missing factors" in your social or romantic life.

The more reassuring the other cards in the spread, the less hesitant you will be to take the first step, whether to clear the air or let someone know that you care.

The less reassuring the situation, or other cards in the spread, the more likely some type of emotional misrepresentation or misinterpretation may be revealed. Discovering where each of you stands in the other's estimation, will make it easier to confront the future, come what may.

Key words:

Crisis or Reward

Card 55

The Ace of Swords, or Daggers.

Tip:

If this card appears in reverse (or upside-down) whether due to matters beyond your control, or poor judgment, you are likely to encounter an unexpected delay, frustration or other emergency.

Card fifty-five means: the possibility of winning or losing even more than you expected in matters.

At your best, you're very conscious of your ability to make or break matters as well as the people who count on you. At this time you may become more intuitive in the company of other people.

Under more stressful conditions however, sometimes an unhealthy mix of ego, temper, and principle, could undermine matters for you at work, at home or both. At other times you may be too easily distracted and waste more time and energy than you can afford.

Card 56 the Two of Swords

Subject Card Two signifies interaction.

There is some uncertainty about a matter at work, at home, or both. You may be waiting for an answer, formulating a reply or preparing to initiate a request or discussion. Despite your desire to be "brave" or "do the right thing" in matters, you're only human. Whether perhaps you're in doubt or under pressure it can be very tempting to do either nothing or to follow the course of least resistance – knowing full well you'll regret it later. Whatever your situation, here's an opportunity to develop a more reliable method to help you cope – whether with situations you can't change, losses that you can't prevent or people that you can't seem to please.

The more encouraging the situation or other cards in the spread, the easier you can play the "waiting-game" in matters now. Any delays you encounter now are more likely to work in your favor strengthening your position as well as your resolve. Whatever the situation (even in medical instances) allowing yourself to take one day, one dream, and one step at a time now can help get you back on course more easily than you imagine. Meditation can help you relax and retain your focus.

The more challenging the situation or other cards in the spread the more challenging it will be for you to remain impartial and patient. Allowing impatience and frustration to control your behavior, or dictate your attitude, could cause you to say and do things that will undermine the cause you are hoping to save, salvage or promote. Whether in the interest of self-preservation or self-advancement, you may even be the instigator of quarrels between other people.

Key words:

Challenging/ Interaction

Card 56

The Two of Swords, or Daggers.

Tip:

If this card appears in reverse (or upside-down) you may suddenly begin to see matters from a more logical, than emotional perspective.

Card fifty-six means: Blind faith and determination tempered with apprehension.

At your best, the more in tune you are with yourself, despite any conflict that may be swirling around you, the easier you can retain your own peace of mind or resolve matters to everyone's satisfaction and best interest – including your own.

Under more stressful conditions however, irrational fears and anxieties may arise when you least expect them.

Card 57 the Three of Swords

Subject Card Three is for thinking and networking.

A matter at work, at home, or both, could pose a challenge to your rationality as well as your agenda. The Three of Swords is often associated with terms such as treachery, sorrow and deceit, which paint a most unpleasant picture. Although it does signal an upcoming delay, disappointment, or loss – more often than not, at least part of our disappointment stems from a matter, person or even one our own talents that we either over-estimated or underestimated. Whatever the situation, the Three of Swords signals a break-down in communications or negotiations that should also trigger a personal wake-up call.

The more encouraging the situation or other cards in the spread, the less surprised you will be by a piece of bad news that you may hear or matters that don't go your way. You may be more relieved that a matter is finally resolved and ready to proceed with an alternative plan of action. In some instances by summoning additional patience and extending a little more understanding you may even re-establish communication or prevent matters from becoming worse.

The more challenging the situation or other cards in the spread the greater your surprise or disappointment will be with a particular outcome, event or person. The more challenging it is to cope with matters, the more important it is not to forsake your faith and hope. Emotional upsets, last-minute cancellations, or a small series of minor misunderstandings at work and home can leave you feeling especially uncooperative, or confused and oversensitive. Talking with a close friend, religious advisor or professional counselor could help.

Key words:

Challenging/Thinking,Networking

Card 56

The Three of Swords, or Daggers
Tip:

If this card appears in reverse (or upside-down) whatever the situation your disappointment may prove to be a blessing in disguise.

Card fifty-seven means: Disappointment. A personal wake-up call suggesting you come to better terms with your inner self and re-adjust your focus.

At your best, you're a deep thinker who tries to consider every genuine and potential aspect of matters before you make a decision or promise. Even if it takes a little longer before you can laugh at some of your mistakes, you learn from them.

Under more stressful conditions however, self-sabotage and/or self-pity can be your greatest enemy. Misappropriation of your time, talent and energy can cause you to repeatedly devise schemes and short cuts that lead to nowhere.

Card 58 the Four of Swords

Subject Card Four stands for incentive and security.

A matter or event at work, at home, or both, will both rejuvenate and restore, or jeopardize your security and motivation. Whatever your situation, you've recently ended or are in the process of concluding a chapter in your life and trying to decide what your next move should be. Whether professionally, medically or emotionally, recouping your energy and regrouping your initiative is a necessary part of this process. Whether you're feeling more or less confident about matters now you'd be wise to avoid any temptation to take matters to extremes, either by trying to do too much or too little.

The more encouraging the situation or other cards in the spread, you have reached a plateau in life, and the more content you are with your location, the more energetically and resourcefully you will work to secure your position, making it easier than ever to resist outside distractions and temptations that might disrupt your comfort zone. The happier you are with your employment, social life or relationship the longer and easier you can hope to maintain your status quo by not jumping to conclusions, making mountains out of molehills or being too quick to assume the worst before you know all the facts in matters.

The more challenging the situation or other cards in the spread the more likely it is that too many matters are hanging in limbo. Whether you're trying to wish a problem away, or believe that you can still save or resurrect a dead issue, denying the facts will do more harm than good. Talking with a close friend, religious advisor or professional counselor could help.

Key words:

Challenging/ Incentive, Security

Card 58

The Four of Swords, or Daggers.

Tip:

If this card appears in reverse (or upside-down) whatever the situation, at the moment your options are likely to be more limited than limitless.

Card fifty-eight means: Limbo. Trying to decide what your next move should be.

At your best, whether you feel as if you're running in first or last place now, you know that accomplishing your dreams and goals is never out of the question. At work and home you approach matters with kindness tempered by wisdom.

Under more stressful conditions however, whenever you're right you'll demand apologies and explanations, but when you're wrong you won't care to discuss matters. Refusing to confront one issue in a timely manner will only complicate if not jeopardize other matters.

Card 59 the Five of Swords

Subject Card Five denotes conflict.

Frustration with matters at home, at work, or both, could incite you to take steps you should have taken before. Impatience or over-confidence in matters could incite you to take unnecessary or foolish risks. The Five of Swords is the ultimate "do-it-yourself" card and like it or not it, can enhance your self-reliance. Whether or not your thought process seems to accelerate you're bound to feel more restless – tense or edgy. Whatever the situation, without even realizing it you could make at least one mountain out of a molehill now.

The more encouraging the situation or other cards in the spread, the easier you can toss aside reluctance or self-doubt to address or proceed with matters you've been wondering or worrying about. Whether or not you're happy with the response, you'll be glad you've brought matters out in the open and wonder why you waited so long. You may begin to exhibit an uncanny ability to calculate the odds when dealing with many people and matters more accurately now, making it easier to identify and eliminate potential problems without becoming distracted. The more determined you are to succeed the more quickly you can learn and apply new methods and tactics that make your task easier.

The more challenging the situation or other cards in the spread the more you need to beware of overstepping your bounds in matters. Whether you've been taking too many matters, people, yourself or your health for granted, you could receive a comeuppance or a response that rocks your world or wounds your pride. Beware of taking unnecessary risks with your health or physical safety. Medically you or someone close to you may be more susceptible to unexpected side effects from medication, or it may prove more challenging for medical authorities to accurately diagnose or treat an ailment or symptoms.

Key word:

Challenging/ Conflict

Card 59

The Five of Swords, or Daggers

Tip:

If this card appears in reverse (or upside-down) whatever the situation you may find it easier to identify the source of your dissatisfaction and come to terms with it if you are ready.

Card fifty-nine means: Controversy. Beware of overstepping your boundaries now in matters at home, at work or both.

At your best, your determination to do the right thing fuels your refusal to take "no" for an answer from yourself and can pave your way to success. If necessary, you may even push aside your fear for yourself and concern for your comfort more easily now to help other people.

Under more stressful conditions however, you can be too easily distracted or annoyed, which could lead to any number of misunderstandings or even an unfortunate accident.

Card 60 the Six of Swords

Subject Card Six challenges and rewards your willingness to keep matters running efficiently and harmoniously.

Whatever your situation "Here we go again" is the key phrase and battle cry for you and the Six of Swords. Your desire to reach a new destination, or achieve a better understanding of yourself, matters or people will require courage. Personally, professionally or medically you've been going in circles and need to unwind. If travel is on your agenda, you may choose to revisit someplace from your past. If travel is not on your agenda, you may have to take an unexpected journey. As long as the quest you choose to pursue broadens rather than narrows your horizons and perspective you can't help but win – though perhaps not in the manner or time frame you expected to.

The more encouraging the situation or other cards in the spread, the easier you can extricate yourself from pointless situations or harmful habits that limit your personal progress and interfere with your ability to honor worthwhile commitments. Whether you need to stop making excuses, or stop accepting them, now is the time to find a better way to handle yourself and matters. Someone that you enjoy may unexpectedly reappear in your life.

The more challenging the situation or other cards in the spread the more likely your true strength of character will be tested. Someone or something may disappoint you – yet again. People, matters, medical or legal issues that you thought were resolved may make an unexpected and unwelcome reappearance. The more vulnerable you are to distractions (especially but not exclusively) from the wrong influences or people the more likely you'll find yourselves having to start over in matters from finance to health and romance.

Key words:

Challenging/ Commitment.

Card 60

The Six of Swords, or Daggers.

Tip:

If this card appears in reverse (or upside-down) whatever the situation the harder you cling to self-defeating habits, thinking or (especially) emotional patterns the more likely you are to repeat the same mistakes.

Card sixty means: you're going in circles and need to unwind.

At your best, you are, patient, steadfast, resilient, conscientious and somewhat cynical. Your preference for handling matters yourself is as inspirational as the resourceful methods with which you can achieve your goals.

Under more stressful conditions however, you can waste too much time, energy and effort believing too strongly in matters and people that are wrong for you and not enough in yourself.

Card 61 the Seven of Swords

Subject Card Seven corresponds to your personal and professional relationships.

Although the Seven of Swords can sometimes imply minor deception, it can occasionally warn you against outright thievery of an object, or from a source that you didn't expect. More often, however, it warns you against stealing from yourself by wasting your time, effort, talents and emotion on non-productive endeavors. Events may put you and other people "on the spot" concerning your integrity or the quality of your relationship.

The more encouraging the situation or other cards in the spread, the easier it will be for you to diplomatically extricate yourself from becoming too involved with matters that don't concern you. Much to your surprise, someone will be less likely to lie to you and more likely to keep a promise or appointment with you. You may be more flirtatious. An opportunity for you to play matchmaker (or be matched up with someone else) could turn out better than you expected.

The more challenging the situation or other cards in the spread the more careful you should be of your possessions, health and safety. Don't be too quick to believe everything you hear, and watch what you say. Something you've said or done could return to haunt you. You may be deceived or a deception that you planned could backfire. The greater the temptation to tell a "white" lie or embellish the truth the more you should resist doing so. The more dependent you have become upon other people's affection or opinions the easier that dependence can sap your strength, erode your individuality, and prevent you from effectively standing up for yourself.

Key words:

Challenging/ Relationships.

Card 61

The Seven of Swords, or Daggers.

Tip:

If this card appears in reverse (or upside-down) whatever the situation you may realize a little sooner than later that you have not fallen as far behind in matters or lost as much as you feared.

Card sixty-one means: Deception. Whether you are feeling overconfident or under confident don't be too quick to believe everything you hear and watch what you say.

At your best, a positive attitude and patience can lend you the additional wisdom and understanding to meet and defeat your problems or detractors.

Under more stressful conditions however, matters can feel more hopeless than they really are.

Card 62 the Eight of Swords

Subject Card Eight stands for renovation.

The Eight of Swords implies a situation that is causing you to feel "bound and tied by circumstances that you can neither prevent nor control". Whether your disposition is surly or sweet, you have the panache and savior fail to appear as if you've resolved matters even when you haven't. Whatever your situation, the longer you wait to confront your inhibitions, or irritation the longer you'll have to settle for just getting by in matters where you could and should have come out ahead.

The more encouraging the situation or other cards in the spread, the more likely your frustration will be of a shorter duration. There will be some extra work, or news coming your way that could upset your day or pre-empt your agenda. You're greatest irritation is likely to stem from the fact that other people waited so long to notify you or to take action.

The more challenging the situation or other cards in the spread, whether you or someone close to you has waited too long to attend a health, personal or professional matter, or you never saw the problem coming, getting matters back on track will require a little more time and effort. The good news is that meeting these challenges is more likely to make you stronger in the long run. If believing that it's no use to try and change your thinking and direction has become a habit, you may be viewing the matters holding you back as "blessings" that give you the strength to shoulder self-imposed burdens. Talking with a friend or perhaps a professional counselor could help.

Key word:

Challenging/ Renovation

Card 62

The Eight of Swords, or Daggers.
Tip:

If this card appears in reverse (or upside-down) whatever the situation you'll have to work harder to prevent matters from overwhelming you.

Card sixty-two means: feeling "bound and tied by circumstances that you can neither prevent nor control".

At your best, at work and home you're uncommonly resourceful when it comes to delegating responsibility and tackling obstacles that could threaten your progress, or security. You can be counted on to devise a logical solution that can resolve any type of dilemma.

Under more stressful conditions however, you can be a willing prisoner and victim of narrow thinking and strong passions – more concerned with today instead of tomorrow.

Card 63 the Nine of Swords

Subject Card Nine represents understanding.

The Nine of Swords implies that at work or at home, consciously or subconsciously you are a slave to anxiety. Whereas some of you may have a strong desire to go into seclusion to escape the confusion in your life, a few of you may simply feel a burning desire to be the best or first in everything, others may be in danger of allowing other peoples problems to consume your life. Whatever your situation, until you realize that your preoccupation is doing you more harm than good, your actions – more than your words, is likely to undermine whatever point you are hoping to make as well as any cause you hope to promote. Confident or unconfident, you can clearly envision what you want, and want to do, but the more important something (or someone is to you) the more challenging it can be for you to face facts. Making yourself take a break now will enable you to recharge your own energy and refresh your perspective.

The more encouraging the situation or other cards in the spread, the more likely you are to realize sooner than later that you're making mountains out of molehills, or laboring under a burden of undeserved guilt. No matter what your situation, you really do have more options than your pride, emotions or principles may be allowing you to consider.

The more challenging the situation or other cards in the spread the more challenging it may be to let other people fight their own battles or live their own life, but you must allow them the freedom to do so. Meditation, yoga, speaking with a religious advisor, close friend or professional counselor could help you.

Key words:

Challenging/ Understanding.

Card 63

The Nine of Swords, or Daggers.

Tip:

If this card appears in reverse (or upside-down) whatever your situation the more willing you are to consider other points of view the more likely you could reach the road to recovery a little sooner rather than later.

SPADE
EPEES

9

SWORDS
ESPADAS

SCHWERTER   ZWAARDEN

Card sixty-three means: Worry.

At your best, you can allow your sense of humor to save the day and your sanity whenever you begin to feel overwhelmed by matters. You can use your experience and compassion to help others help themselves grow through similar trials.

Under more stressful conditions however, getting who or what you want regardless of the consequences can become an unwise – even unhealthy preoccupation.

Card 64 the Ten of Swords

Subject Card Ten is a card for Achievement. It can also generate "instant karma" that can suddenly change the course of events for better or worse.

The Ten of Swords warns you against the folly of committing or continuing to indulge in self-defeating and self-limiting thinking and behavior. Whatever your situation, whether it seems as if everything is happening too quickly or nothing is moving at all, giving in to feelings of over optimism or that you are carrying "the weight of the world on your shoulders" is not in your best interests now.

The more encouraging the situation or other cards in the spread, the more quickly – if not easily – you'll be able to get matters and your attitude back on track by confronting rather than denying your duties and responsibilities. Whatever good news or happy event led to your initial distraction taking a second look at matters now will reveal a few flaws that you weren't willing to recognize before. A second look will also make it easier for you to formulate and follow a more resourceful course of action now, that can still enable you to succeed– as long as you don't decide to give up.

The more challenging the situation or other cards in the spread the harder you may have to work to rejuvenate and redirect your ambition and sense of purpose. Depression can or may be triggering a medical condition that compounds your sense of loss, betrayal or desertion. Pick yourself up, dust yourself off and start all over again. By taking one day and one matter at a time you can begin to recapture your self-confidence, or vanquish that "haunted" feeling and stop victimizing yourself. You also won't be so quick to manufacture reasons to feel suspicious or nervous when matters are going well. Meditation, yoga, speaking with a religious advisor, close friend or professional counselor could help.

Key words:

Challenging/ Achievement.

Card 64

The Ten of Swords, or Daggers.

Tip:

If this card appears in reverse (or upside-down) whatever the situation you may notice some "light at the end of the tunnel" more quickly than you expected.

Card sixty-four means: Despondency. Beware of a tendency to imagine the worst or to create self-imposed restrictions such as, "I can't", "I'm not smart enough" or "I can't do all that."

At your best, you won't give up on yourself and you're always willing to help others who are trying to help themselves. Your ability to combine humor and fact with clever analogies helps you get your point across more effectively.

Under more stressful conditions however, you can be too quick to assume all is lost and burn all your bridges, the moment matters don't appear to be going your way.

CHAPTER 6

Pentacles

Pentacles - Ambition

Keyword: Ambitious Initiative.

Element: <u>Earth</u>

Corresponding Astrological Signs:

♑ Capricorn, ♉ Taurus, & ♍ Virgo

Corresponding Playing Card: Clubs.

Pentacles indicate reaping harvest, breaking new ground, or planting new seeds.

Like the Earth Signs, Pentacles imply establishment, security and continuity. Pentacles are most often associated with financial and professional advancement, material acquisition, material rewards and/or material crisis — factors that also influence personal self-esteem and relationships.

Subconsciously, if not consciously, everything we like or dislike becomes a yardstick by which we measure and judge matters, including our future expectations and ourselves. Pentacles encourage you to keep an open mind, lest you be too quick too discount anything or anyone that doesn't immediately impress you. The more encouraging the situation or other cards in the spread, sooner or later your persistence and effort in matters is sure to be rewarded. The more challenging the situation or other cards in the spread, the more likely economy may have to be your watchword – at least temporarily. The harvest you are about to reap in matters may be less likely to yield as much good as you anticipated, or breaking new ground may prove more challenging than you expected. If the majority of the spread consists of Pentacles, you can expect to encounter varying degrees of fluctuation in either or both your material and personal (or emotional) concerns.

Card 65 the King of Pentacles

Kings can trigger or enhance your personal initiative.

The King of Pentacles can enhance your sense of humor and dependability enabling you to put both to work for your material and professional advantage.

The more encouraging the situation or other cards in the spread, the more likely your financial concerns will flow more smoothly. This could be the right time to apply for a loan – or discover that your loan or credit application has been approved. Now could be the time to seek a promotion or a raise in pay. You might even receive one or the other without asking! Matters at work and at home are beginning to shape up; some are even beginning to yield positive return on the effort you've invested. Meetings or interviews with authority figures are likely to go extremely well. You may get along better with members of the opposite sex than you have for some time.

The more challenging the situation or other cards in the spread, the less generous you and other people will be with one another – at work and at home. You may feel as if everyone you know and everything you're doing is an impediment to your advancement. Since you know this isn't true, try meditating before bedtime. It can help release your inner tension and may reveal the true source of your dissatisfaction.

Romantically, should your spread contain a hint of romance, you may be more inclined to consider settling down. You'll also be more critical of, and selective about, your romantic choices. You may decide to offer or accept a date, declaration of love, or perhaps a marriage proposal.

The more reassuring the situation or other cards in the spread, the more likely it is that you and the object of your affection may embrace a similar type of goal or ambition.

The less reassuring the situation or other cards in the spread, the more likely you and the object of your affection may be too critical or controlling of one another.

Key words:

Ambitious Incentive

Card 65

The King of Pentacles, Coins or Disks

Tip:

If this card appears in reverse (or upside-down) you would be wise to avoid promoting or becoming involved in get-rich-quick schemes, as well as sudden romantic attractions--both are likely to promise more than they will deliver.

RE DI DENARI   KING OF PENTACLES
ROI DE DENIERS   REY DE OROS

KÖNIG DER MÜNZEN   MUNTEN KONING

Card sixty-five means: considering new avenues for advancement and enrichment.

At your best, you exude a quiet sense of dependability that can make you indispensable to even the most independent as well as important people.

Under more stressful conditions however, should you feel that life is turning against you, it could just be that your past is catching up with you.

Card 66 the Queen of Pentacles

Queens can enhance your charisma and people skills.

Whether you're waiting to move on or ahead in life the Queen of Pentacles can enable you use your time more productively.

The more encouraging the situation or other cards in the spread (at work and at home), your patience and clarity allows you to make fewer mistakes. You're willingness to make personal sacrifices, whether for the benefit of others or a larger matter, sets an ideal example. Your ability to drive a hard, but fair bargain wins other people's respect and lends you additional confidence. Now could be the time to seek a promotion or a raise in pay. You might even receive one or the other without asking! You're more appreciative of quality versus quantity. In larger and smaller ways, you're becoming more self-assertive and independent.

The more challenging the situation or other cards in the spread, you may have to become more self-sufficient or accept more responsibility than you feel you're ready (or care to) to handle. Yoga or meditation will help prevent any unresolved feelings of guilt or a tendency to believe that you're being blamed or treated unfairly from triggering a depression.

Romantically, should your spread contain a hint of romance, you may feel more secure about taking a relationship to the next level or more confident about starting over – whether with someone from your past or someone new.

The more reassuring the situation or other cards in the spread, the easier it will be for you and the object of your affection to retain each other's interest.

The less reassuring the situation or other cards in the spread, the more likely you or the object of your affection may speak for the other person without consulting them. This could lead to a difference of opinion about control.

Key word:

Ambitious/Charisma

Card 66

The Queen of Pentacles, Coins or Disks.

Tip:

If this card appears in reverse (or upside-down) beware of becoming too sure of yourself, or too fond of power and material possessions.

REGINA DI DENARI   QUEEN OF PENTACLES
REINE DE DENIERS   REINA DE OROS

KÖNIGIN DER MÜNZEN   MUNTEN KONINGIN

Card sixty-six means: Achieving bottom-line results and answers is your main objective.

At your best, you have a deep loyalty to your goals and apply strict concentration to your methods. Your competent manner gives the impression that you can handle anything and your positive example inspires others to follow your lead.

Under more stressful conditions however, meddling in others' affairs—under the guise of acting in their best interests is more likely to work against your best interests.

Card 67 the Knight of Pentacles

Knights indicate unexpected developments in matters or your behavior.

Each Knight has the potential to trigger a different type of behavior. The Knight of Pentacles can enhance your patience for working out the details in matters that pertain to your economic and emotional growth and stability.

The more encouraging the situation or other cards in the spread, the easier you can begin planning ambitious long-range projects such as beginning or expanding your own business, buying or selling a home, or gathering data to secure a promotion or better job. At work and at home, your logical approach can move mountains while minimizing the danger or effects from smaller rockslides of opposition. You're particularly aware of your duties and responsibilities and take great pride in accomplishing everything to the best of your ability.

The more challenging the situation or other cards in the spread, the more suspicious and critical you'll be of even the best advice or information. Forcing yourself to make decisions because you choose to believe you have no choice will cause you to make choices you'll regret.

Romantically, should your spread contain a hint of romance, you could become involved in a secret love affair or become involved in a group activity that could lead to better romantic opportunities. Socially and romantically, you're less likely to be as interested in pursuing or continuing relationships with people who simply want to "live for and in the moment."

The more reassuring the situation or other cards in the spread, the more likely you and the object of your affection will prefer getting together in quiet surroundings, rather than, a rambunctious night on the town. **The less reassuring** the situation or other cards in the spread, if you're not behaving like a wet blanket, you may feel as if your partner is.

Key words:

Ambitious/ Adventure.

Card 67

The Knight of Pentacles, Coins or Disks.

Tip:

If this card appears in reverse (or upside-down) whatever your situation, any reluctance on your part, to take action in matters before it's too late may result in ongoing problems at home, at work – or both.

CAVALLO DI DENARI   KNIGHT OF PENTACLES
CHEVALIER DE DENIERS   CABALLO DE OROS

RITTER DER MÜNZEN   MUNTEN RIDDER

Card sixty-seven means: taking a logical approach now, can move mountains and minimize the danger or effects from smaller rockslides of opposition.

At your best, personal mediocrity is an unacceptable alternative in your eyes.

Under more stressful conditions however, you can become too pessimistic or disinclined to do more than necessary to get someone or something to leave you alone.

Card 68 the Page of Pentacles

Pages signal small matters with the potential to grow larger.

The more encouraging the situation or other cards in the spread, the stronger your attraction to people and matters that are more sensible than sensational. You may become more interested in pursuing hobbies and entertainments that serve a more practical than idealistic purpose. You may even pursue the possibility of turning a hobby into a full-time job. This is a good time to consider whether or not to have a child (or another child) because you're better equipped to determine the advantages and disadvantages.

The more challenging the situation or other cards in the spread, the more challenging it will be for you to gain even a slight advantage or break in matters at work and at home. This is not a good time to consider whether or not to have a child because whatever you decide is likely to be for the wrong reasons. You could make small financial or emotional miscalculations that can rapidly snowball into a major inconvenience or disagreement.

Romantically: Should your spread contain a hint of romance, this time period could mark a significant turning point in your emotional and social development.

The more reassuring the other cards in the spread, becoming involved or more involved in events sponsored by your community or place of worship could be the first step towards a more rewarding social life, as well as the opportunity to meet someone new with similar material goals and emotional values. Should you have a current date mate or partner, now may be the time to begin taking small steps towards planning a more permanent future together.

The less reassuring the situation, or the other cards in the spread, the easier and more quickly your, (or your partners) head could be turned by people that appear to promise more than they intend to deliver.

Key word:

Ambitious/ Surprises.

Card 68

The Page of Pentacles, Coins or Disks.

Tip:

If this card appears in reverse (or upside-down) beware small miscalculations that could rapidly snowball into a major inconvenience or disagreement.

FANTE DI DENARI   KNAVE OF PENTACLES
VALET DE DENIERS   SOTA DE OROS

BUBE DER MÜNZEN   MUNTEN SCHILDKNAAP

Card sixty-eight means: a small opportunity to gain some type of advantage – that others might overlook or consider too much work.

At your best, the more practical and realistic you are, the easier you can transform a losing matter into a winning proposition.

Under more stressful conditions however, you may become irrationally obsessive, paranoid and secretive.

Card 69 the Ace of Pentacles

Aces represent crisis or reward.

At work and at home, the more encouraging the situation or other cards in the spread, the more likely some type of opportunity will literally fall into your lap. Purchasing or selling property, job promotions, better job offers, residence changes, redecorating your home, inheritances, legal settlements and "lucky wins" all fall under the jurisdiction of the Ace of Pentacles. Someone may repay a small amount of money they borrowed from you. You may be relieved of a financial obligation.

The more challenging the situation or other cards in the spread, the more likely you are to encounter an unexpected and unwelcome financial burden or delay. Repairs as well as ordinary expenditures may prove more costly than you anticipated, or you may become so preoccupied with one person or matter that you ignore everything else.

Romantically: When it comes to romance, finance is often interwoven with Ace of Pentacles. Should your spread contain a hint of romance, the opportunity to meet someone new may soon be yours in any number of mundane ways, ranging from a change in your employment, (or work schedule) to making the simplest purchase – or costly repair! Long-time couples may begin making plans for a new child, home, vehicle or honeymoon.

The more reassuring the other cards in the spread, better your chances to obtain, retain or recapture material security and emotional stability.

The less reassuring the situation, or the other cards in the spread, personal spending habits, or excessive professional responsibilities may each play a role in either complicating or dismantling long term relationships as well as short-term attractions and infatuations.

Key words:

Crisis or Reward.

Card 69

The Ace of Pentacles, Coins or Disks.

Tip:

If this card appears in reverse (or upside-down) you are more likely to encounter and unexpected financial expense or delay.

Card sixty-nine means: an opportunity that could fall into your lap or a dilemma that could prove to be a blessing in disguise – possibly even one of each!

At your best, you can be relied upon to minimize the danger from others' mistakes, carelessness, inexperience or egotistical blundering.

Under more stressful conditions however, the more ambitious you are the more manipulative you can become.

Card 70 the Two of Pentacles

Subject Card Two signifies interaction.

In addition to balancing our budget and schedule the Two of Pentacles also represents our never-ending quest to balance the past and the present to accommodate our hopes for a brighter future. The more adaptable you are now, the easier and more quickly you can adjust to the ups and downs that would otherwise complicate your daily routine. Best of all, with the Two of Pentacles it's not unusual for romantic, financial, or even legal opportunities as well as a stroke of unexpected good fortune, to crop up when and where you least expect them.

At work and at home, the more encouraging the situation or other cards in the spread, the easier it will be for you to juggle matters on your agenda. This is a good time to review and possibly restructure your economic future – focusing on long range benefits. It's easier for you to separate the essential from the non-essential issues in your life and recognize your priorities. Your persistence only accentuates your irresistability. You can talk anyone into giving you a bargain, a break or another chance. Multi-tasking is your specialty now and each project you complete flows effortlessly into the next, thus, allowing you to accomplish more to your satisfaction in less time than usual.

The more challenging the situation or other cards in the spread, the more susceptible you'll be to citing a real or imaginary illness as a means of avoiding matters and people that you don't want to face. Financially, you may need to "rob Peter to pay Paul" for a little while. When matters aren't going as you intended or hoped, try to remember that fate isn't trying to punish you – but push you in a better direction.

Key word:

Ambitious/ Interaction

Card 70

The Two of Pentacles, Coins or Disks.

Tip:

If this card appears in reverse (or upside-down) at work and home matters that begin moving at a slower pace may give you time to catch your breath and catch up with other projects.

Card seventy means: multi-tasking can (or may need to) be your specialty now.

At your best, you can talk anyone into giving you a bargain, a break or another chance.

Under more stressful conditions however, unrealistic thinking may result in irritability, depression, or feeling as if you're riding an emotional seesaw.

Card 71 the Three of Pentacles

Subject Card Three is for thinking and networking.

Although the Three of Pentacles is particularly favorable for anyone who is about to launch a well planned endeavor or ready to take an established job or relationship to the next level, it strongly favors those who are ready to begin seeking or rebuilding a better life for themselves.

At work and at home, the more encouraging the situation or other cards in the spread, the more direct and decisive your thought pattern and communication will be. You're more interested in delivering and receiving bottom lines than idealistic speculation. This is a good time to conclude matters, projects or studies you've been working on because you can clearly see what will and will not work for you. You'll be more inclined to save than spend your money. You're also more efficient and creative. This is a good time to rearrange your cupboards or dig into gardening. People will be dealing with the "real" you.

The more challenging the situation or other cards in the spread, the more likely you may feel that what you have is holding you back from acquiring what you want or deserve – especially if your personal life has become cluttered with too many insecure or needy personalities. You may accuse someone else (or they may accuse you) of material or emotional misrepresentation. This isn't the time to start a new class, job or project because either you won't enjoy it or grasp the subject matter as quickly as you expected. Everyday travel may prove more to be more complex, costly and/or frustrating than usual.

Key words:

Ambitious/Thinking, Networking.

Card 71

The Three of Pentacles, Coins or Disks.

Tip:

If this card appears in reverse (or upside-down), the feeling that something is missing in your life seems to be undermining your ability to relax or the quality of your performance at work, home or both. Now may be a good time to re-examine your goals.

Card seventy-one means: whatever your situation, you can clearly see what will and will not work for you now.

At your best, you call upon your strengths to conquer your weaknesses rather than disguise them.

Under more stressful conditions however, you can become too shortsighted, stubborn or unforgiving.

Card 72 the Four of Pentacles

Subject Card Four stands for incentive and security.

The Four of Pentacles reminds you that no matter how hard you hope or try, you simply can't have matters both ways. Whether you've become too stingy or too free with your emotions, time or material resources the more willing you are to compromise with matters (and other people) in the near future the more you stand to gain in the long-run. The more possessive you are the harder it will be to compromise with whatever changes are on your horizon and the longer you will feel as if your back is to a wall.

At work and at home, the more encouraging the situation or other cards in the spread, the more you're ready to "dig-in" and do whatever needs to be done – confident that you can handle what may come. This is a good time to cautiously explore any offers or possibilities that could lead to new or better employment. At work, home or both you'll be perfectly content to take the time you need to complete matters to your specifications. Your approach and handling of people and matters is quite realistic and mature, bringing you closer to people you care for about.

The more challenging the situation or other cards in the spread whether you had expected them to or not, other peoples' problems can become yours overnight. This may include the burden of caring for someone else. Your company or employer could encounter setbacks that pose a threat to your job security or income, or perhaps it's time to come to grips with an emotional or medical issue of your own. Whatever your situation, allowing your frustration with any type of intrusion or the circumstances that caused them could handicap your desire to tend to matters as quickly as you should.

Key words:

Ambitious/ Incentive, Security

Card 72

The Four of Pentacles, Coins or Disks.

Tip:

If this card appears in reverse (or upside-down) you may soon discover that whatever you're trying to hang onto is costing you more than it's worth.

Card seventy-two means: you can't have matters both ways.

At your best, you can do your best work under pressure – from meeting deadlines other people would consider impossible to pulling other peoples ideas together in a manner that benefits everyone.

Under more stressful conditions however, self-awareness (or self-concern) can limit your objectivity and lead you blow matters completely out of proportion.

Card 73 the Five of Pentacles

Subject Card Five is a card of conflict.

With the Five of Pentacles your emotional and material concerns are a little more complex because they are so interwoven. The greater your concerns the greater your inner turmoil and the easier that turmoil could affect your better judgment, undermine your physical health or even trigger a freak accident or a close call. The more in touch you are with your Faith, dreams or intuition the more easily you can you make choices in matters that are right for you.

At work and home, the more encouraging the situation or other cards in the spread, the more likely it is that one or two matters are either not going to go your way or move as smoothly as you had hoped. The good news is that they won't cost you as much time or money as they might have. You are also going to learn a valuable lesson through these matters, perhaps, about trying too hard. If you've been under too much pressure lately (self-induced or otherwise) and this is a good time to "pamper" yourself as much as you can afford to.

The more challenging the situation or other cards in the spread, the more likely you may feel as if everyone is simply too demanding – especially your loved ones, no matter what their age. Taking the slightest risk with your safety or finances could produce dire consequences. This is NOT the time to borrow or loan money. It may seem as if it's simply one delay after another in matters. Everything about your work will become more challenging and a little less enjoyable. Medically, your system may find it as challenging to deal with a cure as an illness. Whatever your situation, remaining focused upon the "bigger picture" or the greater good will help you help yourself to surmount your challenges more quickly.

Key word:

Ambitious/Conflict

Card 73

The Five of Pentacles, Coins or Disks.

Tip:

If this card appears in reverse (or upside-down) you may find it's becoming easier to appreciate and develop your own talents without cost to your emotional focus.

Card seventy -three means: Hardship. One or two matters are either not going to go your way or move as smoothly as you had hoped.

At your best, you can walk away from arguments that you could win – when you know the issue is pointless

Under more stressful conditions however, you may blame your professional problems on your personal life and your personal problems on your professional life.

Card 74 the Six of Pentacles

Subject Card Six challenges and rewards your willingness to keep matters running more effectively, smoothly and harmoniously.

With the Six of Pentacles the more confidence you have in your abilities the easier you can attract the attention of people who can advance your interests. Although waste not want not should be your motto you'd still be wise to carefully examine any and all opportunities or requests that might come knocking at your door. If not, you could pay a higher price than you expected.

At work and home, the more encouraging the situation or other cards in the spread, you're going to tackle your daily routine with a renewed sense of vigor and purpose. A legal matter may soon be resolved in your favor. You may receive some type of bonus or recognition for a job well done. However, your determination to bring order into chaos wherever you go could be a double edged sword if you overstep your bounds. The more you hope to accomplish, the more you need to pace yourself, because you may tire more quickly now. You may become more conscientious about your physical health or change your sleeping habits to better accommodate your energy and work schedule.

The more challenging the situation or other cards in the spread, your health or sleeping habits may suffer from nervous tension due to problems at work and/or at home. You may be reaping the consequences of your own or someone else's financial neglect, irresponsibility or immaturity. Whatever you're employment or routine, you're bound to wish you were doing something different. However, if you quit or lose your employment now, it may be harder to find something new. Should you find new employment now, your wages may not meet your expectations or settling in won't prove as easy as you had hoped. In a short while, you'll be able to use the lessons that you're learning the hard way now to help you chart a better path.

Key words:

Ambitious/Commitment.

Card 74

The Six of Pentacles, Coins or Disks

Tip:

If this card appears in reverse (or upside-down) faulty judgment may add additional complications to your complex emotional and financial network.

Card seventy-four means: waste not, want not.

At your best, at work and at home, no detail is too small to escape your full attention. You can transform virtually any task into an inspirational adventure. The busier you are the better you feel, and the more you can accomplish.

Under more stressful conditions however, your determined approach may generate a little friction in some of your relationships.

Card 75 the Seven of Pentacles

Subject Card Seven corresponds to your personal and professional associations.

Whether for better or worse, other people are going to encounter a different aspect of your personality, because the Seven of Pentacles can signal a self-identity crisis, that leads you to take a closer look at endeavors and relationships into which you have been investing the majority of your time, money and emotions. The less satisfied you are with your efforts the more challenging it will be to continue seeing only what you wish to be true. The more satisfied you are with the results of your labors, the less reluctant you will be to seek or accept new and better opportunities to expand your horizons.

At work and at home, the more encouraging the situation or other cards in the spread, the more likely you and other people are to gain a new sense of respect for one another. Your resourceful behavior and attitude will generate positive attention and perhaps some timely introductions to people that can benefit you. The busier you have to be, the easier it will be for you to conform to a more efficient behavior pattern, making it easier to clear away any and all clutter that is (or has been) standing in the way of your progress.

The more challenging the situation or other cards in the spread, any negativity, resistance or confusion you encounter (no matter how small) could be "the last straw" that causes you to take your irritation out on other people. You could nurse a grievance or worry completely out of proportion especially (but not exclusively) if any aspect of a loved one's life or earning potential is in jeopardy.

Key words:

Ambitious/ Relationships.

Card 75

The Seven of Pentacles, Coins or Disks.

Tip:

If this card appears in reverse (or upside-down) you may need to seriously consider seeking additional income or reconstructing certain aspects of your relationships at home, work or both.

DENARI
DENIERS

7

PENTACLES
OROS

MÜNZEN   MUNTEN

Card seventy-five means: self-identity crisis.

At your best, your ability to remain focused on the positive and important aspects of any project or relationship can prevent you from being overwhelmed by trivial concerns.

Under more stressful conditions however, the more challenging it is to confront or express your own feelings, the more quickly you can begin to expect the worst in matters or imagine that others' are being untruthful or conspiring against you.

Card 76 the Eight of Pentacles

Subject Card Eight stands for renovation.

The more comfortable you are with your abilities, the easier you can grasp "the big picture" in matters now and simply sort out the details as you go. Whatever changes, challenges or obstacles you're about to encounter will only invigorate you and strengthen your determination to succeed. The less certain you are about what you want to have or do the longer you will remain one of life's professional students – always claiming to know more than everyone else but accomplishing less than anyone else.

At work and at home, the more encouraging the situation or other cards in the spread, the more self-assertive and focused you will be upon what you want to achieve and what you need to do to make it happen! Just be sure to provide an adequate explanation for postponing other matters. You'll want to devise ways to increase your material holdings. You may begin to play a more active role in guiding any current investments you have. You may consider taking a second job or explore self-employment. You may begin a private savings account or investment as a "just in case" measure. You may receive a promotion on your current job or begin to interview for a higher-paying position. You may also want to invest in your health and take confident steps towards preserving or improving it.

The more challenging the situation or other cards in the spread, some type of emergency could either deplete your ready cash or threaten your savings account. You may begin to realize that the future of your job or company could be in jeopardy. A medical problem for yourself or someone close to you could prove to be more serious than you suspected. No matter how challenging the circumstances, take heart. Meeting these challenges is helping you transform former weaknesses into personal strengths.

Key words:

Ambitious/ Renovation.

Card 76

The Eight of Pentacles, Coins or Disks.

Tip:

If this card appears in reverse (or upside-down) what was once your "comfort zone" may begin to feel more like a rut that is preventing you from making the most of yourself.

Card seventy-six means: everything that you deem a priority will receive your full attention and co-operation. Your recent achievements may speak for themselves and you as well!

At your best, a ready and willing worker with excellent powers of organization and leadership – no task is too large or small to merit your full attention and consideration.

Under more stressful conditions however, you can become too focused upon petty grievances and resentments that limit rather than broaden your horizons. You may seek self-gratification in any number of self-indulgences.

Card 77 the Nine of Pentacles

Subject Card Nine represents understanding.

As long as you understand that protecting your material resources is secondary to protecting yourself from self-delusions that can impede your better judgment, the Nine of Pentacles can be one of the most fortunate cards in the Tarot. Should you be expecting too much from matters or other people, or allowing them to demand too much from you, reality may puncture your fantasy.

At work and at home, **the more encouraging** the situation or other cards in the spread, the more benefits you stand to gain – thanks to your past perseverance and unwavering faith. You may discover that you have a secret admirer. You may receive a nomination, an award, reward, party, promotion or just sincere thanks and recognition at home, at work or from your community. Family or business connections could prove fortunate for you in some way. You may soon purchase or inherit property. From finance to romance and everything in between (such as diet or health concerns– seeking a better job, redecorating your house or updating your appearance) now's the time to stop "talking" about what you want to do and simply do it! Your determination to "get on with your life now" will help you transcend your former uncertainty, procrastination, unhappiness or fear of rejection.

The more challenging the situation or other cards in the spread, the more likely you are to hear news and gossip that is not only hard to believe but may be rather unkind or unfair to you as well! Think carefully before you retaliate, share secrets or pass along gossip or rumors because something you say now could come back to haunt you later. You may attract and be attracted by entertainments and people that could bring you more trouble, danger or heartache than they will be worth – especially (but not only) if you are grappling with some type of emotional disappointment or loss.

Key words:

Ambitious/ Understanding.

Card 77

The Nine of Pentacles, Coins or Disks.

Tip:

If this card appears in reverse (or upside-down) you may need to guard against financial loss or material damage, or perhaps even a threat to your reputation and integrity.

Card seventy-seven means: whatever your situation, personal achievement is your best means of attaining genuine peace of mind.

At your best, you possess great strength of character and purpose. You're as efficient as you are self-sufficient—able to enjoy others company and still be perfectly comfortable by yourself.

Under more stressful conditions however, the easier you can lull yourself into a false sense of security.

Card 78 the Ten of Pentacles

Subject Card Ten is a card for Achievement. It can also generate "instant karma" that can suddenly change the course of events for better or worse.

At work and at home, **the more encouraging** the situation or other cards in the spread, people who have more of what you want will motivate you to set your sights higher while those who have less will inspire you to count your blessings! You might get lucky playing the lottery with friends, family or co-workers. You will attract and be attracted to other people that are concerned about their future and you may discuss or share information about taxes, inheritance, insurance policies and savings programs. Your employer may announce plans for future expansion or some other program that will stabilize your position. If you are self-employed, it could be easier than you expected to branch out or sell your current business. You're likely to feel either a little more romantic or nostalgic. You need to feel that the people you care for care about you and realize that you are always there for them.

The more challenging the situation or other cards in the spread, the more you may need to take better care of your physical health. You, or a loved one, could develop problems with or allergies to foods or conditions that never bothered you before. If you or a loved one has had an ongoing medical condition it could require more attention now. You may be required to take or share someone else's financial responsibility. Problems for your company or between you and your employer could pose a threat to or end your employment. If you're not turned down for any type of credit or loan you may have to pay an exorbitant interest rate. Much to your chagrin, whatever the cause for the moment, economy will have to be your watchword.

Key word:

Ambitious/ Achievement.

Card 78

The Ten of Pentacles, Coins or Disks.

Tip:

If this card appears in reverse (or upside-down) you'd be especially wise pay closer attention to the people and matters that mean the most to you.

Card seventy-eight means: Obligation. Feeling or taking a greater sense of responsibility towards other people and matters.

At your best, your ability to radiate humor, peace and commonsense may make it almost impossible to determine where your friends begin and family ends.

Under more stressful conditions however, you may become so involved in others lives that you lose track of your own affairs.

CHAPTER 7

Ready to Read

Before we plunge into working with an actual Tarot spread, we need to briefly discus two other topics: Signature Cards and Timing Events.

Signature cards

I prefer to read without using a signature card, but do a few readings with them before you decide. The traditional Celtic Cross Tarot spread will require that you select a signature card. Our Tarot-Dynamic Celtic Cross does not. Signature cards are most often assigned in one of three ways — age, physical attributes or corresponding astrological element. People with blonde hair are represented by the King or Queen of Cups, according to their gender. People with red-hair are represented by the King or Queen of Wands. Brunettes are represented by the King or Queen of Pentacles. Older people are represented by the King or Queen of Swords. Men under the age of twenty-five are most often represented by the Knight that corresponds to their Astrological element. Women under the age of twenty-five are generally represented by the Page that corresponds to their element.

When selecting a signature card, you can devise your own method, use the traditional selection, or even select a card from the Major Arcana if you wish. For instance, if you're reading for a woman who is hoping to become married you might select Card 19 — the Sun, or even Card 50 — the Ten of Cups, to represent her. You'd probably select the King of Pentacles to represent a businessman. Don't forget though, that each of us has our very own signature card that corresponds to our astrological element. The signature card for the Fire Signs: Aries, Leo or Sagittarius is the King or Queen of Wands. The signature card for the Earth Signs: Taurus, Virgo and Capricorn is the King or Queen of Pentacles. The signature card for the Air Signs: Aquarius, Gemini and Libra is the King and Queen of Swords. For the Water Signs: Pisces, Scorpio and Cancer, the signature card is the King or Queen of Cups.

Timing events

Timing events can be a challenge. As a rule, the more strongly I "feel" a matter in relation to a particular Tarot card, the sooner and more likely the event seems to come to pass. Eventually, you will "feel" this too. Bear in mind that I say, as a rule, and rules are made to be broken.

Some time ago I did a series of what I felt were excellent – even inspired readings. I did not hear from the client again for a year and a half. When they contacted me they requested another reading as quickly as possible! After that urgent reading, they disclosed that they had enjoyed our previous sessions but were extremely disappointed when nothing that I had alluded to came to pass.

However, they said, in the last week there been a sudden change for the worse at their place of employment. They then accidentally came across the recordings from our first two sessions. Hoping to take their mind off their troubles they played one tape after the other — and there I was describing in great detail exactly what had occurred and was happening NOW. Long ago I stopped trying to rationalize how that episode came to pass. It has happened a few times since with different clients, so hearing this may prove helpful to you.

Timing and the minor arcana

There are also times when what we see and feel is as perplexing for us as it is for the person for whom we're reading. So, first of all be honest, let the person know that you cannot state a definite time frame with absolute certainty. Since your debate is more likely to be between one or two cards from the Minor Arcana, pay attention to their suits.

Let's pretend you're doing a reading in mid-May, which is the time of Taurus. Your puzzlement stems from a Wand. Wands equal Fire Signs and times. The next time of fire would be Leo, which runs from the 23rd of July to the 23rd of August. After Leo, there won't be another Fire time until Sagittarius, which runs from November 23rd to the 21st of December. If the time period between now and Leo feels right, consider telling the person: "I feel this event will come to pass in between now Taurus, and Leo, July, August. If Leo doesn't "feel" right but you're not sure, consider telling them: "Although this could come to pass between now Taurus, and Leo, July, August, I'm more comfortable stating a time frame between Leo, July, August, and Sagittarius, November, December".

Should your timing dilemma stem from two cards within the same suit of the Minor Arcana, say Cups for example, consider the following. It's still mid-May. The next time of Water would be Cancer, after that comes Scorpio, then Pisces in the early portion of the next year. Chances are good the event will come to pass between Cancer and Scorpio of this year, but if you're not comfortable making that pronouncement, expand your time frame saying: "Between Cancer June-July of this year and Pisces, February-March of next year".

Timing guide

Aries = Fire = Wands	March 21 to April 20
Taurus = Earth = Pentacles	April 21 to May 20
Gemini = Air = Swords	May 22 to June 21
Cancer = Water = Cups	June 22 to July 22
Leo = Fire = Wands	July 23 to August 23

Virgo = Earth = Pentacles	Aug. 24 to Sept. 22
Libra = Air = Swords	Sept. 23 to Oct. 23
Scorpio = Water = Cups	Oct. 24 to Nov. 22
Sagittarius = Fire = Wands	Nov. 23 to Dec. 21
Capricorn = Earth = Pentacles	Dec. 22 to Jan. 20
Aquarius = Air = Swords	Jan. 21 to Feb. 18
Pisces = Water = Cups	Feb. 19 to March 20

Timing and the major arcana

In matters of timing Major Arcana cards can be particularly tricky. In most readings their role and nature is more spiritual or psychological than worldly. Whenever possible, I rely on Minor Arcana cards when timing events. However, there are those who prefer to read only the Major Arcana cards. I can't say they're wrong if it works for them.

For me, though, to perform a reading using only the Major Arcana Cards would be like reading half the story. There are many Tarot books available in bookstores and libraries. The majority of them contain remarkable — even lavish (though sometimes confusing) detail, especially concerning the Major Arcana. Each Major Arcana card is purportedly ruled by a combination of two or more planets. Unfortunately, there are as many combinations as there are authors to devise them. So if you decide to use only your Major Arcana to perform a reading, my suggestion is to leave the timing to your intuition.

CHAPTER 8

One Card Personal Guidance

Enabling you to see the <u>big</u> picture in matters

This simple technique is an excellent method for reducing stress, enhancing your focus, and enabling you to see the "big" picture in matters. This technique can be particularly enlightening if you perform it during your favorite part of the day, whether you're a morning person, day-timer or a night owl. If you've recently been feeling irritable or restless for no real reason, separating the Major Arcana cards from your Tarot deck and selecting a card from the Major Arcana may help you discover what your inner self is trying to tell you. However, if you're seeking spiritual reinforcement because your life is going well, somewhat unsettling, or simply going nowhere, using the entire Tarot deck is the best idea.

Relax. Take your time. Shuffle your cards in any manner you wish, while concentrating upon a place or activity that you enjoy, such as walking along a beach or through a forest. When you're ready, fan your cards across the tabletop and select one from anywhere in the deck, but before doing so study them for a moment.

Although you may use either hand to select your card, consider using your left hand as it is closest to your heart. Let your hand drift above all the cards before making your choice. When you do this, don't be surprised if you're eye or your hand feels drawn to one particular section of the cards. If so, it's perfectly normal and you will probably make your selection from there.

However, it's also perfectly normal if you don't always feel an attraction to one particular card or section of cards. Remove the card of your choice from the deck and place it face up in front of you. If it appears upside down please place it right side up.

This card's definition offers suggestions to help you handle yourself and matters.

If you've selected a card from the:

Major Arcana: = personal transformation. The matters you're grappling with are karmic in origin. This cards definition offers suggestions that can replenish your peace of mind.

Wand: = Change. This cards definition offers suggestions that can assist you in making or adapting to changes more easily. It may even help you avoid making hasty changes that you could regret.

Cup: = Emotion. This cards definition offers suggestions that can heighten your awareness, enrich your creativity or help prevent your emotions or imagination from running away with you.

Sword: = Challenge. This cards definition offers suggestions that can replenish your courage and determination.

Pentacle: = Ambition. This cards definition offers suggestions that can help you increase or re-establish your security. It may also help you minimize or withstand a material dilemma.

CHAPTER 9

Three Card Spread

Personal enlightenment

Whenever I feel the need to read my own cards, this is my favorite spread. Why? Because it tells me what I need to know and can do – without jeopardizing my objectivity. If your concerns revolve around your inner self, whether re – affirming your self-control or a question about your health you may wish to read for yourself using only the cards from the Major Arcana.

However when other matters and questions prompt you to seek spiritual reinforcement, use your entire deck of Tarot cards. Ready? We're going to repeat the same procedure that we used to select one card. Relax. Take your time. Shuffle your cards in any manner you wish while concentrating upon a place or activity that you enjoy, such as walking along a beach or through a forest.

When you're ready, fan your cards across the tabletop, selecting <u>three</u> cards from anywhere in the deck, but before doing so study them for moment. Let your left hand drift above all the cards before making your choice. Remember it's perfectly normal if you're eye or your hand sometimes feels drawn to one particular section of the cards and it's normal if you don't always feel a particular attraction to any one section of cards. Remove the cards of your choice from the deck and place them face up in front of you. If it appears upside down please place it right side up.

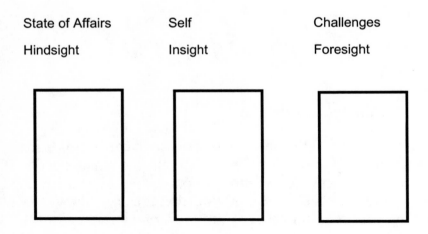

State of Affairs   Self   Challenges

Hindsight   Insight   Foresight

Now before you begin to retrieve each card's definition, study the cards, recall our formula and see what "feelings" you receive from the cards you selected.

MAJOR ARCANA CARDS = Personal Transformation. Major Arcana Cards test, reward, and replenish your strength of character.

WANDS = Change. Wands can promote changes that lead to personal renewal by helping you accept the necessity of making some changes and adapt to others.

CUPS = Emotion. Cups signify whether your desire and ability to believe in and work towards a brighter tomorrow is a little stronger or weaker now.

SWORDS = Challenge. Self-control can transform the ideas and challenges that you initiate as well as encounter into an opportunity to succeed.

PENTACLES = Ambition. Pentacles are most often associated with financial and professional advancement, material acquisition, material rewards and/or material crisis.

CHAPTER 10

Tarot-Dynamic Celtic Cross Spread

Doing a reading for someone else

The Celtic cross may be the best known and most popular of all the Tarot spreads. It is an excellent spread with which to do a reading for someone else. Once you become more familiar with your Tarot cards, and more confident about interpreting them, the seeker may not need to ask their question out loud. For now, however, allowing the seeker to ask you what they wish to know will help you remain focused and allow you to see more of what they need to know.

Simple questions are best. For example, "I've been concerned about a work matter", or "I'm hoping to move", or even "How's my love life?" Invite them to ask one question. If you don't, they may produce a list, which would intimidate even the most adept Tarot reader. The less they say, the less inhibited you'll feel and the more you'll see in their cards. Let them ask their question before they begin to shuffle the cards.

If you're using a signature card please select it from the deck after the seeker asks their question and before they begin to shuffle the cards. Place it right side up on the table facing you, in the position of Card number 1 and focus on the seeker's signature card while they relax, think pleasant thoughts and shuffle the rest of the deck.

If you are not using a signature card, the card that will occupy the first position will provide helpful clues concerning whatever the seeker needs to know. Either way, ask the seeker to relax and think pleasant thoughts while shuffling the cards. Encourage them to take their time and shuffle the cards in any manner they wish until they feel ready for you to read them.

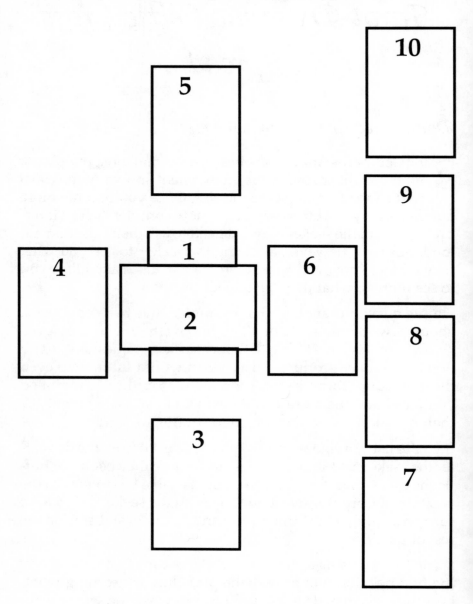

When the seeker is ready, you may begin to lay out the cards according to the diagram. Let the story that you have to tell them flow naturally. Take *your* time. Their question may have been about purchasing a new car, but you're going to see much more than a black and white yes or no. You may, for example, also see a new job, a promotion, a residence change or unexpected company arriving.

Although they may be planning on purchasing that new car next week, you may see and sense a delay – whether an unexpected bill or the fact that they can't comfortably afford the purchase right now. Tell them what you see and feel through the cards. You may not always be able to tell people what they want to hear, but you'll always be able to tell them what they need to know. Many times people are merely seeking unbiased affirmation of something they already know.

Don't be afraid to let them record your session. One or more things that you say today that they can't immediately relate to are likely to become perfectly clear in a matter of weeks or a couple of months.

Here is a placement and referral guide to the Celtic Cross to help you get started.

The prompts for Card Number 1 contain more detail than the prompts for Cards 2-10 because:

Card Number 1 suggests the seeker's reasons for having the reading.

Major Arcana: You are in a period of personal transformation and self-awareness.

Wand: You have been encountering many changes in matters and people lately.

Wand Court Card: You are, or are about to become more self-assertive and may be luckier than you realize, if you don't become too overconfident.

Wand Subject Card: You have been contemplating the wisdom of making some changes.

Cup: You have been more emotional and/or reflective lately.

Cup Court Card: Your feelings and intuition are more intense now. Whether for better or worse, your feelings are altering your emotional perspective and behavior.

Cup Subject Card: You're daydreaming, wishing, hoping, wanting to know but afraid to ask where matters are going.

Sword: You are, or will need to become more focused upon an important matter.

Sword Court Card: You are in a state of fluctuation. One moment you believe you can't lose; the next you believe you can't win. Even so, you are very determined, whether to pursue a new goal or finalize an old one.

Sword Subject Card: You are at a crossroads about how to best handle a person or situation.

Pentacle: You are concerned about your material stability or emotional security – maybe both.

Pentacle Court Card: Emotionally, materially or both you are striving to put down new roots.

Pentacle Subject Card: You need to consider weeding your circumstantial garden. Some matters need more sun; others need more shade.

Card Number 2 states why it's likely to be a little easier or more challenging for the seeker to handle what comes successfully.

Major Arcana: The upcoming matters are karmic. The happier you are with yourself now the more quickly and surely you will resolve any problems that could arise. The less satisfied you are with yourself or your life now the longer matters will remain in limbo until you are willing to consider an alternative course of action.

Wand: Matters may prove more challenging but meeting them will cause you to feel more alive. Flexibility is the key to making the most or best of whatever changes you set in motion as well as any that could take you by surprise.

Cup: The stronger your emotional objectivity the more accurate your intuition, so the sooner you will recognize the "bigger picture" and the less likely you are to fool yourself or be fooled by others.

Sword: Much will depend upon your frame of mind. The greater your determination to succeed the sooner you will transform potential stumbling blocks into stepping-stones. The longer you choose to remain focused on the problem instead of seeking a logical solution the longer you will remain a victim of circumstance.

Pentacle: The upcoming matters will provide opportunities for you to reap some rewards, while tackling some additional or overdue duties and responsibilities. The more focused you are upon getting ahead in life the right way the less wasteful you will be with your time and resources.

Card Number 3 outlines the heart of the matter; where the seeker stands or what they need to know more about.

Major Arcana: you are at a turning point concerning your past and future goals.

Wand: approaching changes at home, at work or both.

Cup: emotional concerns.

Sword: tension or instability at home, at work, or both.

Pentacle: concerns about your personal and professional status and ambitions.

Card Number 4 suggests that either a past event or a personal habit that could be influencing the seeker's present concerns or behavior.

Major Arcana: You've been feeling yourself and your life changing in ways that you didn't expect. Perhaps you believe you've received a circumstantial wake up call. Then too, maybe peace of mind has always seemed to elude you.

Wand: A desire to broaden your horizons or put more distance between yourself and matters (or people) that you can see will never change. Or, perhaps you have always feared rather than welcomed change – except on your terms.

Cup: Happy or sad recollections have been causing your imagination to run away with you lately. Then too, perhaps viewing people and matters, as you want to see them instead of as they really are has always posed a problem.

Sword: The circumstances, under which a cause or goal was won or lost. Or, perhaps, a tendency leap before you look may simply be a habitual part of your behavior.

Pentacle: A recent increase or decrease, in your job status or material holdings may be spurring your drive for advancement. Then too, sound money management may have always posed a problem for you.

Card Number 5 suggests what the seeker could achieve but also needs to beware of.

Major Arcana: Achieve: Truth. Beware: Self-Doubt.

Wand: Achieve: Self-renewal, flexibility and independence. Beware: Personal burn-out.

Cup: Achieve: Peace of mind. Beware: Procrastination.

Sword: Achieve: Inspiration and self-control. Beware: Self-righteousness.

Pentacle: Achieve: Greater opportunity. Beware: scattering your energies and wasting your resources.

Card Number 6 outlines conditions and matters in the near future.

Major Arcana: events at work or at home will test your character.

Wand: sudden gains or opposition may come from nowhere.

Cup: an emotional time period.

Sword: a stressful time period.

Pentacle: time for a reality check.

Card Number 7 outlines the seeker's self-doubts

Major Arcana: failure/mediocrity.

Wand: inability to make or cope with change.

Cup: disappointment or loneliness.

Sword: opposition or retribution.

Pentacle: loss of security or reputation.

Card Number 8 outlines what the seeker stands to learn or gain from matters.

Major Arcana: understanding, enlightenment.

Wand: happiness.

Cup: peace of mind.

Sword: courage.

Pentacle: security.

Card Number 9 suggests the type of impact that the seeker's interactions with other people can have upon the situation.

Major Arcana: independence, confidence and constructive self-assertion.

Wand: the opportunity to branch out and become more resourceful.

Cup: new awareness and appreciation of yourself and others.

Sword: more constructive self-expression and effective bargaining techniques.

Pentacle: stability and resolution; to know where you stand in matters.

Card 10 presents the bottom line for the entire reading

Remember: a more challenging outcome card simply means you have a little more work ahead.

Major Arcana: you're ending an old chapter and entering a new phase in life.

Wand: you're on the brink of a very active, and adventurous if somewhat hectic time period.

Cup: you're undergoing an emotional and possibly spiritual transformation.

Sword: your greatest challenge will be to remain focused upon your ultimate goal.

Pentacle: Approach the future optimistically yet, realistically.

CHAPTER 11

Determining Whether One Suit Holds The Majority

Good reading versus Great reading.

Now we are going to address and answer the age-old question of which cards in a Celtic Cross Spread are the most important. Here are five pertinent examples and comprehensive guidelines that can transform a "good" reading into "great" reading.

EXAMPLE ONE

Upon looking at the complete layout you see that three out of ten cards are Kings. The more Kings there are in the spread the more important your past and present relationships with men or authority figures will be to your progress. This indicates that whether or not you'd expected to, you're likely to hear from, about, or be in contact with more men than usual for whatever reason. No matter what cards accompany those three Kings, the Kings are the focal point of the reading so the circumstance they represent will prove more significant to the seeker's future. The other cards will reveal more of what you need to know concerning the nature or outcome of this contact. Three or more of *any* identical Court Card (three Kings, three Queens, three Knights, three Pages, three Aces) constitutes a majority.

EXAMPLE TWO

Upon looking at the complete layout you see that five out of ten cards are from the Major Arcana. The more Major Arcana

Cards there are in the spread the more emotionally or spiritually significant this reading will prove to be. This indicates that you are at, or are approaching, some type of turning point. No matter what cards accompany those five Major Arcana Cards, they are the focal point of the reading and the circumstance they represent will prove more significant to the seeker's future. The other cards will reveal more of what you need to know concerning your transition or the reasons for it and possibly both.

Five or more of *any* Major Arcana Cards (Numbers 1 -22) constitutes a majority.

EXAMPLE THREE

Upon looking at the complete layout you see that six out of ten cards are Sword subject cards. If the majority of the spread consists of Swords, your greatest challenge will be to remain focused upon your ultimate goal. This indicates that whether or not you'd expected to, you're about to encounter one or more distracting situations. No matter what cards accompany those six Swords, they are the focal point of the reading and whatever circumstance they represent will prove more significant to the seeker's goals and future.

The other four cards will reveal more of what the seeker needs to know concerning the reasons for this distraction and what options they have. Three or more of *any* Subject Cards from the same suit constitutes a majority.

EXAMPLE FOUR

Now let's mix n match. Upon looking at the complete layout you see that three out of ten cards are Subject Number five cards. The more fives you find throughout your reading, the more adversity or temptation you are about to confront. You also see that three out of the remaining seven cards are Cups. If the majority of the spread consists of Cups, the matters at hand may prove to be more complex than they appear, or your manner of handling them may be more emotional than the matter itself. No matter what cards accompany those three Number Five cards and three Cup cards, they form the focal point of the reading and the circumstance they represent will prove more significant to the seeker's future. The accompanying cards will reveal more of what you need to know concerning the situation. Six or more of <u>any</u> combination (3 and 3) constitutes a majority.

EXAMPLE FIVE

Occasionally, the first card (which represents the seeker) and the last card (which represents the outcome) will not only be from the same suit they will also be the only representatives of that suit. This reading marks the beginning of a time period that will initiate a permanent change in the seeker's handling or direction of life – and whatever the seeker's concerns it will take longer for them to be resolved to the seeker's satisfaction. Should the first and last card be the only representatives from the:

Major Arcana; matters may not be completely resolved for a year or longer.

Minor Arcana; whether or not the seeker is aware of it they are about to embark upon a very tumultuous time – period in accordance to the basic keyword for the suit itself.

If the first and last cards are subject cards, pay attention to their numbers as well. For instance a reading that begins with:

Card 30 the **Four of Wands** and ends with Card 31 the **Five of Wands** could indicate a particularly busy and possibly quarrelsome time period at work, home or both.

Card 42 the **Two of Cups** and ends with Card 50 the **Ten of Cups** could indicate that a proposal of marriage, or a child or even a new home is on the way. However, depending upon the accompanying cards, it could also indicate reconciliation after a misunderstanding or meeting someone completely new.

Card 57 the **Three of Swords** and ends with Card 51 the **King of Swords** could indicate loss of a job that may lead to a better position with a better employer or even self-employment. Then too, some type of disagreement could result in legal action; or consulting a specialist may avert a serious medical issue.

Card 76 the **Eight of Pentacles** and ends with Card 70 the **Two of Pentacles** could indicate that the seeker is not as materially astute as they imagine. Whatever they are hoping for may not materialize as quickly as they hope, expect or deserve.

Whatever the situation, encourage the seeker consult the cards again in about 3 months.

In my experience, an easier or more "encouraging" reading consists of a wide variety of suits and numbers. The more times one particular suit or number is repeated the more "challenging" the circumstance they represent and the more significant that circumstance will be to the seeker's future. Do not mistake the word "challenge" for "catastrophe".

Being diagnosed with any illness is a challenge but not always a catastrophe. Making a job or career change is a challenge. Receiving a political nomination poses a major challenge. However, situations such as these and many others often trigger a turning point for the better in a person's life. With a little time and practice you're sure to devise your own guidelines.

CHAPTER 12

Horoscope Spread

Readings for a birthday present

You can do this spread anytime you wish but when you do, take notes. You'll be amazed at how accurately your Tarot Cards outline the prognosis of the coming months – especially if you treat yourself — or someone else to this reading for a birthday or at the start of the New Year!

After you relax and shuffle your cards feel free to arrange the cards in any pattern you wish! If, (for example) your birthday falls in July you can choose whether to begin your reading by allowing Card Number One to represent July or August. If you have a question in October about next March you can choose

January	February	March	April	May	June
1	**2**	**3**	**4**	**5**	**6**

July	August	September	October	November	December.
7	**8**	**9**	**10**	**11**	**12**

whether to begin your reading by allowing Card Number One to represent October or November.

Before you retrieve each card's definition, take a moment to study the cards, and see what "feelings" you receive from the cards you selected.

MAJOR ARCANA CARDS = Personal Transformation. This month you'll be doing some soul-searching.

WANDS = Change. Wands blaze their own trail and this portends an adventurous or busy month ahead.

CUPS = Emotion. An emotional month at home, work or both that could improve your communication and understanding with yourself and other people too.

SWORDS = Challenge. Self-control is the key to transforming any challenges or delays that you encounter this month into an opportunity to succeed.

PENTACLES = Ambition. A good month for prioritizing, making and finalizing plans as well as setting yourself and matters in order.

The Author

Anna Burroughs Cook has been reading and interpreting the Tarot for 30 years and has developed a wide base of clients across the United States as well as throughout Ohio and in Lorain County area where she currently resides.

She has appeared on Television and radio programs and taught private classes including Tarot and Psychic Development classes in Adult Education programs. Tarot-Dynamics has been well received by students, educators and Tarot enthusiasts for its accuracy and ease of use.

Taught and lectured

TV Evening Sports News with Paul Warfield — November 1979

TV Afternoon Exchange — Dec 1980

Private Class in Tarot and Psychic Development — April 1981

Lecture Series for Adult Education on Tarot and Psychic Development — 1983

Adult Education on Tarot and Psychic Development at Rocky River High School — 1984

Private Class in Tarot and Psychic Development Parma Ohio 1985

Radio Appearance on WCPN 90.3 FM National Public Radio — October 2000

Author & Teacher of "Tarot-Dynamics" — April 2003

Interviewed By Lane Strauss for Cleveland Magazine – October 2003

Private Class in Tarot and Psychic Development — October 2007

Kima Global Publishers, an independent publishing company based in Cape Town, specialise in *Books that Make a Difference to People's Lives.*

We have a unique variety of Body, Mind and Spirit titles that are distributed throughout South Africa, the U.K., Europe, Australia and the U.S.A.

Among our titles you will find non-fiction, healing, wellness, philosophy, parenting, business coaching, personal development, creative workbooks and visionary fiction.

Our books are printed and sold all over the world!

Look out for our counter bookstand with our body, mind & spirit pocket range.

Our address is:
Kima Global House
50 Clovelly Road

Clovelly

Cape Town 7975

South Africa

www.kimaglobal.co.za
www.bodymindspiritbooks.net
www.wisdomcavebooks.com

Look out for our counter cards stand with our Tarot deck range.

Kima Global Publishers distribute the wonderful range of Lo Scarabeo Tarot decks in South Africa. Please visit our web site for more information.

If you enjoyed this book (and naturally we hope that you did) we recommend the following titles for your further reading enjoyment.

The Language Of Light
By **Nadine May** *mind drawing through the higher self*

With an accompanying Meditation pocket book on the Qualities of our Soul energy

OUR FIRST 48 SOUL QUALITIES, WE ALL HAVE WITHIN US, COME ALIVE THROUGH OUR MEDITATION!

ISBN
0-9584493-8-4

ISBN **0-9584493-3-3**

This creative workbook, making your own card deck, is full of mind–drawing exercises that will guide the reader into their own inner worlds. It also explains the chakra system and how it resonates with our thought-patterns.

The character Tieneke (from the awakening novels) is the narrator of this workbook.

In Nadine's first awakening novel Tieneke teaches these art-analogue mind-drawing classes in order to activate the Language of the Soul.

Nadine has successfully combined truth with visionary symbolic art techniques by teaching mind drawing techniques to awaken the Language of Light, the language of the Soul. This first awakening workbook will be a breakthrough for many during their initial stages of awakening. When the Light quotient in our being is 33% we feel as though we are opening up our inner senses. Telepathy, clairvoyance and clairaudience etc. seem normal and natural to us.

LaVergne, TN USA
15 October 2010
200903LV00001B/76/P

Finding the Textbook You Need

The IVP Academic Textbook Selector
is an online tool for instantly finding the IVP books
suitable for over 250 courses across 24 disciplines.

---

ivpacademic.com